I0901871

LOST TREASURES *of* HOUSTON

William Dylan Powell

Copyright © 2025 by Reedy Press, LLC

Reedy Press
PO Box 5131
St. Louis, MO 63139, USA
reedypress.com

No part of this publication may be reproduced or transmitted in any form or by any means, electronic or mechanical, including photocopy, recording, or any information storage and retrieval system, without permission in writing from the publisher.

Permissions may be sought directly from Reedy Press at the above mailing address or via our website at reedypress.com.

Library of Congress Control Number: 2025936461

ISBN: 9781681066059

Cover images: (*top left*) courtesy of HHRC, (*top right*) courtesy of HHRC, (*second row left*) courtesy of Michael Martin, (*second row right*) courtesy of the author, (*third row left*) courtesy of HHRC, (*bottom left*) courtesy of Michael Hart, (*bottom right*) courtesy of Library of Congress

Images courtesy of author or believed to be in the public domain, unless otherwise noted.

Printed in Canada

25 26 27 28 29   5 4 3 2 1

DEDICATION

This book is dedicated to every Houstonian who's ever said: "You know, I remember when all of this was nothing but trees/cattle/prairie/crops/swamp."

Houston Astrodome
Courtesy of Library of Congress

TABLE OF CONTENTS

San Jacinto High School
Courtesy of Wikimedia Commons

ACKNOWLEDGMENTS

Big thanks to the staff of the Houston History Research Center, the University of Houston Libraries, the Texas Historical Commission, and the Texas Medical Center. Special thanks to everyone who took the time out of their days to share their thoughts on which *Lost Treasures of Houston* they felt were most worthy of note. This includes Bethany Andell, Grace Rodriguez, Kirk Eggleston, April Lundy, Amorette Quintanilla, Wade Cady, Ariel Heiblum, Christian Milam, Jeanne Perdue, Janeen Comer, Shannon Winton, Cindy Heywood, Sarah Gish, Julie Fischer, Deborah Braund, Bela Adela, Mary Ann Harvey, Mike Barker, Kelly Coleman Jasper, Kris Lee, and many others.

Special thanks to those who shared their memories, stories, and photos, including Candace Garcia, Kevin Trotman, Lauren Sedlar, Michael Hart, Meredith Symonds, Edouard Dubiton, John Beeman, Ron Hellman, Curtis Cameron, the crew at Roznovsky's Hamburgers, Sarah Pacilio, April Vega, the crew at GenerAsian Radio, the very generous folks at Andre's Confisserie Suisse, David Chien, Sharon Leibman, Amanda Pape, J. R. Delgado, Leon Beck, Frank Patin, Charles Rodriguez, Gerry Nicodemus, Jose Luis Rayo, Benjamin Herarra, Travis L. McIntire, Cheryl Czerewaty, Whitney Andrews Corson, Mario Pina Fuentes, Robert Boyd, Houston legend Bruce Godwin, Brian Merzbach, Lawyer B. Douglas II, Babette Hale, Ron Stone Jr., Kristi Jay, David Greif, Kevin Bakos, Dave Meeks, and Robert Snoza. Not all of your photos made the final edit, but all of your efforts were very much appreciated.

Special thanks for the support of my lovely Aunt Brenda; my wife, Stephanie, who basically ran the house while I was doing this; and, of course, my parents, Bill and Jeanette Powell.

Howard Hughes

Courtesy of Library of Congress

INTRODUCTION

Confession: I got a little down for a few weeks writing this book.

After all, I had *so many* personal memories of these now-gone places. Golfing at Bear Creek Golf World with my father. My mom taking me back-to-school shopping at Foley's. Fancy celebrations at Charley's 517. Cheering on the Oilers for many years. Tuning in to Marvin Zindler for the slime report. Now, all of these things and so much more: gone. Vanished faster than the first bowl of Chuy's Creamy Jalepeño Dip.

I suspect these pages will dislodge your share of memories too. You likely have your own stories to tell about Westbury Square or the Wilde Collection or the *Houston Post* or Radio Music Theatre. But my blues didn't last and, hopefully, neither will yours. These experiences connect you to the city and all the rest of us. We're in this together. Through all of us these people, places, and phenomena live on. Even the ones we don't want, like the back-to-back 1–13 seasons the Houston Oilers had in 1972 and 1973.

There's a pace to this place. We don't stand still for long, and not just because of the mosquitoes. Change is as much a fixture here as allergies and that one guy who drives into the flood puddle thinking he can make it. So as many lost treasures as I shared here, there just wasn't room for it all in these pages. Like a hungry alligator that's not quite right after spending too much time in the Ship Channel, the years have gone crazy and snapped up countless things this city has loved. There was just too much. Maybe we'll do another edition. In fact, email dylan@houstonwriter.com and let me know what I should add next time around.

I hope you enjoy *Lost Treasures of Houston* and that it stirs up a lot of fun memories. That's really what this book is about. I meant it to be a Felix queso-soaked homage to Houston's past; a sentimental Gilley's hat-tip to the H-Town of yesterday smelling vaguely of vinyl records and cigarette smoke; a high-humidity time machine transporting us back to when cop cars were still Columbia blue—and I still had hair. If you think this book does any of that, please consider leaving a review or sharing it with a friend. I'll see you in the past!

{FOOD and DRINK}

When I casually mentioned this book to friends and family as I was writing it, I noticed an amusing pattern. The first thing each person did was to mention one of the big, iconic treasures of Houston's past, such as the Houston Oilers or AstroWorld or maybe something like the big Gulf Lollipop sign, if they were of a certain age. But the second thing each did without fail was to rattle off a list of now-defunct restaurants and bars they once loved the approximate length of Interstate 10, complete with their favorite entrées. Each and every person did this—more than a dozen people, at least. Fun fact: People *really* liked the Old San Francisco Steakhouse.

It's not surprising that I'd get a lot of feedback on the feed bag. According to the Greater Houston Partnership, there are almost 12,500 restaurants in the area—not to mention 650 food trucks and around 100 wine bars. There are more than a hundred delis. Nationally, Houston ranks among the nation's top 10 cities for restaurant spending. All that means two things are true: There are a lot of restaurants, and they have to be really, really good to even stand a chance. And yet, these things simply have a lifespan. So you can do everything right, and a restaurant still eventually runs its course—true of many we've included.

Houston has also lost many fine bars and breweries over the years, including neighborhood institutions. Many people think of Gilley's first and foremost. Kay's Lounge was a popular suggested topic; according to photographer and longtime patron Meredith Symonds, that Texas-shaped table still makes the odd

Gulf Brewing Company

The Old Spaghetti Warehouse
Courtesy of the Texas Historical Commission

appearance at special events. Houston's hippie-era past can be found by looking back at the swinging days of Dome Shadows. And, of course, there were all the places on Richmond Avenue that featured fake smoke and might randomly play New Order's "Bizarre Love Triangle" at any moment, like City Streets or Bayou Mama's.

For me, personally, the Richmond Arms and Blanco's were painful to lose. Stick around long enough and you tend to collect long-lost favorites like leaflets under a windshield wiper. So let's pull up your reservation and take a tour of Houston's bygone tables and taverns.

Ye Olde College Inn
Courtesy of HHRC

Ding How Owners
Courtesy of HHRC

Barry's Pizza and Italian Diner Sign
Courtesy of Sarah Pacilio

Bud Bigelow's Restaurant

RESTAURANTS

That celebratory post-Rice-football-game dinner at Ye Olde College Inn. Fried chicken and biscuits at the San Jacinto Inn after a family outing at the monument. We make restaurants such a part of our lives, but when the final course is over, they flip the Closed sign around, and all we have left is a doggy bag of memories. And maybe high cholesterol. Still, leftovers can taste pretty sweet. From the four-star to the French fries, let's reheat a few good times from some of Houston's lost dining establishments.

Courtesy of Boston Public Library

Felix Mexican Restaurant

The Felix Mexican Restaurant chain opened way back in 1937. Owner Felix Tijerina didn't ride the wave of growing Tex-Mex popularity—he helped create it. The 904 Westheimer location (1948) would become the local chain's flagship. Houstonians grew to crave its classic dishes, such as enchiladas drenched in chili con carne, fresh-made tamales, and a creamy queso recipe that, in hindsight, should probably have been classified as a Schedule 1 narcotic. Tijerina had six restaurants at the height of the business and went on to become a local civic leader. The Westheimer location shuttered in 2008.

Spaghetti Warehouse

Courtesy of Lisa Lagman

Opening in 1972, Houston's downtown Spaghetti Warehouse with its checkered tablecloths, trolley car, and generous portions helped transform Market Square. The historic Desel-Boettcher Building at 901 Commerce was not only a popular dinner spot but also supposedly one of the most haunted places in town. Hurricane Harvey washed out the restaurant's 40+ year run, though technically the business still operates Warehouse 72 out of the Marq-E Entertainment Center. Post-Harvey the building was sold and renovated, becoming McIntyre's Downtown for a few years. As of this writing it's now a 3-in-1 club called El Centro.

Courtesy of HHRC

San Jacinto Inn

Founded in 1916, LaPorte's San Jacinto Inn offered fresh, all-you-can-eat fried chicken, seafood, and homemade biscuits. In the 1920s, the restaurant charged just $1 for its buffet. Hugely popular, it served more than a million oysters per year at its peak. Practically everything on the menu was deep fried and deeply delicious (I researched this firsthand back in the day). But more health-conscious trends meant the end of the place in 1987. Today the nearby Monument Inn offers the same sort of experience, serving a buffet honoring the beloved old restaurant. Sure, it's not exactly the same, but the Monument Inn's exceptional cinnamon rolls do take the sting off a bit.

Le Viet

Courtesy of Lauren Sedlar

Houston arguably has the best Vietnamese cuisine outside of Vietnam, with the possible exception of certain parts of California. From a modest strip center on the west side, Le Viet at 11328 Westheimer Road quietly grew a huge following lasting more than a decade. A stylish interior and exceptional service made for a great experience when paired with Le Viet's diverse menu of pho, Vietnamese crepes, Mekong soup, Bun Bo Xao Cha Gio (lemongrass beef), spicy tamarind chicken, and a lot more. The complimentary shrimp chips were so good you forgot you had more food coming. The good news? The owners now run Que Huong in Hong Kong City mall, which Houstonia magazine called "the city's best Vietnamese restaurant."

Los Troncos

Courtesy of Vintage Pickers

Many restaurants offer private rooms. But only Los Troncos at 1516 Westheimer placed its private rooms in a tree. Yep, Los Troncos (The Trunks) served grown-ups dinner in a real-life treehouse. What in the ever-loving live oak was happening over there? The odd but upscale restaurant featured 19 individual treehouses in which patrons could dine. Founder Victor Sears had lived in Mexico for a decade, owning several restaurants there before opening Los Troncos in Houston in the swinging—from a tree, if you have a mind—'60s. The menu was all over the place, ranging from lobster to chicken curry. Despite its trendiness and popularity, Los Troncos fell in the late '70s.

Mama's Cafe

Mama's on Westheimer was all about comfort food. The original opened in San Antonio in 1981—you can still find them in the Alamo City. For around 30 years, though, Houston patrons settled in under the kitschy Texas diner decor for breakfast burritos, cold beers, chicken fried steaks, greasy burgers, "Huevos Hoffbrau," rib eyes, and more. Mama's was not beloved by foodies. It was beloved by people who wanted a loud, lively breakfast with friends or family. The place was always packed—often by those who'd had a long night but weren't quite ready to go home. (It didn't close until 4:30 in the morning.) Last call for the Houston location, however, was in 2012.

Ye Olde College Inn

Courtesy of Boston Public Library

Founded by George Martin (no, not the *Game of Thrones* guy) in 1920, Ye Olde College Inn at 6545 South Main became unofficial headquarters for Rice athletics, complete with a "coach's table." It was designed by William Ward Watkin, the original campus architect. The menu was upscale and eclectic, though Ye Olde College Inn could always be trusted for a great steak. It was more expensive than your average college hangout, and parents often treated their kids during a visit. A recipe book published by the second owner, Ernest Coker, sported dishes such as chicken Valencia, stuffed flounder, oysters Burgundy, and pumpkin-bourbon pie. Historians are unsure whether the bakers at Ye Olde College Inn served up as many turnovers as the Rice Owls on any given Saturday.

PIG STAND

Reputedly the world's first drive-in restaurant chain, the Pig Stand was founded in 1920s Dallas. Pig Stand #7 at 2412 Washington Avenue was Houston's first. It made an impression with pastel colors, little pig figurines, table jukeboxes, and a menu ranging from burgers to trout. Unsurprisingly, its go-to was a barbecue "pig sandwich." Pig Stand #7 actually featured in the *Terms of Endearment* sequel *The Evening Star* (1996), in which Bill Paxton goes on a cheap date with Shirley MacLaine. The Washington location shuttered in 2006, with the franchise's last location in San Antonio closing for good in 2023.

Courtesy of Kevin Trotman

One's a Meal

Courtesy of DL

Today most people automatically associate this lost treasure with Greek food, but that wasn't always the case. One's a Meal was originally a sandwich shop opened in 1920 on Rusk Avenue. The name alluded to the size of the sandwiches. The business grew to more than 20 locations. But by 1978, when Haritos Bibas purchased the business, only the West Gray location remained. Bibas slowly added Greek items to the menu (along with a helluva chicken soup, I have to say). Bibas eventually sold the business, running Bibas' Diner out of the West Gray building, but it would shut for good by 2012. Not many restaurants can say they had such an impressive stretch, though.

The Green Parrot

Opening in 1952, the Green Parrot's Houston restaurant was the fourth in the Kansas franchise. Named after an actual bird kept at one of the other locations, the Green Parrot operated out of a beautiful neocolonial mansion at 2314 Macgregor Way. Famous for fried chicken, it also served up other comfort foods, such as steaks, catfish, shrimp, tossed salads, huge bowls of green beans and mashed potatoes, Parker House rolls, and those congealed Jell-O desserts that would today more than likely prompt someone to call the Department of Homeland Security. The business changed owners and locations in later years before closing in 1967. No word on whether the parrot caused the restaurant to run short on crackers.

Roznovsky's Hamburgers

This beloved burger-and-chili stop at T. C. Jester in Oak Forest was as much about community as it was the uncommonly good burgers and French fries. The place had a homey feel with game mounts, gimme caps, and UT baseball memorabilia decking the walls. Owner Ron Roznovsky was a talented baseball player who brought home championships for UT and even played in the minors. The restaurant opened in 1986, though the family also owned a small grocery store in Rice Military for a time. After Roznovsky's passing in 2015, the restaurant closed and the building became a Tacos A Go Go.

Courtesy of Roznovsky's Hamburgers

The Strawberry Patch

Founded in 1976, the Strawberry Patch was the first of many beloved Houston restaurants brought to us by the Pappas family. I loved this cozy, effervescent place that served classic American fare. It sported a huge wooden bar in the middle, and the whole interior was adorned with wicker chairs, so much brass it felt like a *Price Is Right* showcase from the Bob Barker years, overhead Tiffany lamps, live plants, and pretty much everything you'd find in the casual grill of any respectable country club at the time. But ask anyone who went there what they remember most, and they'll probably mention the fresh, complimentary muffins delivered to every table. The Strawberry Patch closed in 1993.

Courtesy of Cihan Yuce

Joe Matranga's Italian Restaurant

A WWII Navy veteran, Joseph Matranga was a man of many talents—among them cooking and singing. After the war, he opened a bar with his brother. When some patrons suggested that Houstonians might pay real money for his delicious homemade pasta and sauce, he bought his brother out, and in 1947 Joe Matranga's Italian Restaurant was born. For decades, the restaurant at 3700 Irvington Boulevard with its classic checkered tablecloths and wax-dripping chianti bottles was Italian food in Houston. It ran until 1990. Matranga took the exact ingredients of his pasta sauce with him to the great sauce pan beyond but left quite a legacy.

Bellaire Broiler Burger

Broiler Burger opened in 1959 at 5216 Bellaire Boulevard. Originally called Brittain's Broiler Burger, it was the third local restaurant in C. L. Brittain's chain. The concept was burgers cooked like you make them at home—only without singeing off your eyebrows. An ad announcing the grand opening read, "See 'em Broiling Over Real Charcoal." Burgers came with crinkle-cut fries. The restaurant's interior sported no-frills Formica tables and simple booths and, for a while, reportedly even a Conestoga wagon for the kids. The place earned a loyal following that lasted decades, changing owners a few times before the flames went out for good in 2022.

Licensed under CC 0 Universal Public Domain

Las Alamedas

This one really hurts. The old Las Alamedas near Interstate 10 and Voss was a fine Mexican dining experience like no other. Firstly, the stucco hacienda-style building was enormous—almost 15,000 square feet. It was replete with beautiful Mexican antiques, a massive bar, and a relaxing wooded view out back. The overall effect was opulent but not stuffy. And the food was fantastic, offering tasty Tex-Mex fare along with upmarket seafood options and decadent desserts. In 2009, a dispute with the landlord meant relocating to Katy. The new location was nice enough, but Las Alamedas closed permanently in 2020.

Confederate House

Houston wasn't a cattle town like many Texas cities; it was a Southern town. And the Confederate House, established in 1948 on San Felipe, did its best to preserve Old South culture in the Bayou City. Waiters in white tuxedos served shrimp cocktails, prime tenderloin, broiled red snapper, prime double lamb chops, and of course, "Confederate Fried Steak." Proper attire was enforced, and John the bartender never forgot a patron's drink. For decades, the city's great and good dined at Confederate House. The restaurant moved several times, and rebranded beyond its Southern heritage, before closing in 2008. Ladies were not required to wear a curtain rod (belles of a certain age will get that one).

Kaphan's

Founder Eli Kaphan turned a cow pasture at 7900 South Main into one of the most upscale seafood restaurants in town. His menu offered individual baby red snapper in a remoulade sauce, Florida lobster with shrimp cocktail, a phalanx of steak options, and much more. Kaphan was a former baseball player and collector of sports memorabilia, so the restaurant often sported interesting odds and ends from the baseball world. One of the specials was grilled Miami Marlins (kidding). In addition to the menu, an elegantly designed building with white tablecloths and a crackerjack wait staff helped give Kaphan's about a 70-year run before closing its doors in the 1990s.

Photo courtesy of Boston Public Library

Congo Jungle

Photos courtesy of Boston Public Library

Exotically flavored nightclubs were all the rage in the mid-20th century as a result of tiki culture influence, Hollywood romanticization in films such as *The African Queen*, and the rum-soaked popularity of musicians like Les Baxter and Martin Denny. From 1946 to 1962, the Congo Jungle at 5704 Almeda Road was all over this trend. Started by Abe Jamail, known as "Houston's most decorated war hero" for his service in WWII, the Congo Jungle offered live music every night among an exotic backdrop of palm trees, foliage, and mural-covered walls featuring jungle beasts. The wait staff even sported leopard-print dresses. It's the perfect restaurant theme for Houston, where only the strong survive during rush hour, and sometimes you have to carry your own water during hurricane season.

Ding How

Courtesy of Boston Public Library

This wasn't the first Chinese restaurant in town, but it was among the earliest. Ding How's building at 6800 South Main was considered exotic for its day, as was its cuisine. Ding How was owned by the successful Gee family. Albert Gee learned the restaurant trade from his uncle, opening a few smaller enterprises before Ding How. Though the local Chinese community had its own traditional tastes, Ding How served dishes designed to appeal to American diners, such as barbecued pork, chop suey, and egg foo young. The Gee family continues to be a prominent presence in the Houston community through its many philanthropic endeavors including the Gee Family Association Education Fund of Greater Houston, the Gee Family Association, significant donations to Rice University, and much more. Today, Tripadvisor alone lists more than 270 Chinese restaurants in the Houston area.

Ship Ahoy

The Houston location of this small Southern franchise first sailed into town in 1935. Originally at 1007 South Main, the restaurant resembled a yacht on land even more than the Cadillacs of the day (which got as long as 20 feet). Ship Ahoy promoted itself as "Houston's most exclusive restaurant," sporting a menu including all manner of regional broiled fish such as flounder, snapper, and Gulf shrimp—as well as dozens of popular seafood dishes like trout almondine and filet of sole sauté meuniere. They could also hook up non–seafood lovers with steaks, lamb chops, chicken, and even Italian and Chinese food. The restaurant moved to 6638 South Main before finally running aground in the 1960s.

Sambuca

In the heart of downtown at 909 Texas Avenue, Sambuca opened in 1998 at the corner of Travis and Texas on the ground floor of the Rice luxury apartments (formerly the historic Rice Hotel). Known for its upscale and chill ambiance, Sambuca was a go-to place for dinner, drinks, and dancing. A combination of out-of-town talent and local jazz regulars played Sambuca, including the Yellowjackets, the Watercolours, Acoustic Alchemy, the Blue Monks, Yvonne Washington, and many more. The restaurant closed in 2024 after a 26-year run, citing Houston's rising crime and homelessness, as well as fallout from COVID-19 mandates.

FINE DINING

Once the oil started flowing, it didn't take long for Houstonians to crave an evening of fine dining. Charley's 517 was a conservative classic. The Great Caruso on the west side kept the "dinner and a show" tradition alive for years. Maxim's on Lamar was among the first fancy-shmancy Houston restaurants with dishes like lobster thermidor and red snapper excelsior. Joe Mannke's Rotisserie for Beef and Bird set exceptional standards in wild game. Vargo's was a special occasion destination for decades. And the pretheater crowd clamored for Damian's with its Shrimp Damian and *costoletta alla valdostana*.

Courtesy of Pixabay

Charley's 517

Located at 517 Louisiana Street, Charley's is still what I think of when I imagine a nice restaurant. Waiters wore tuxedos. The classically trained European chefs were world-class, serving French nouvelle and other cuisines with fresh ingredients and artful presentation. And the wine list? Amazing. Today, some might find all that stuffy. And, indeed, in its later years Charley's did loosen its double-Windsor-knot tie a bit. But today people wear pajamas to the grocery store, so perhaps Houston has swung too far in the other direction. A number of headwinds, including catastrophic downtown construction, forced Charley's into Chapter 11 in 2003. But nobody can take away the champagne toasts and fine memories that exceptional old restaurant gave so many Houstonians.

Courtesy of Umpteen Postcards

Vargo's

Vargo's at 2401 Fondren was the kind of place you went to celebrate something special in Houston, like weddings, anniversaries, or the first day after summer in which nothing in your car melted. Its verdant, beautifully landscaped property totaled almost nine acres and featured bright azaleas, a quaint gazebo, a private lake, and a generous flock of wild peacocks that meandered around the place (peacocks roam many neighborhoods on the west side). The menu was conventionally Continental with things most children refuse to eat, like escargot, lobster bisque, veal scallopini, and the like—but people really came for the charming atmosphere. Founder Al Vargo sold the business in 1996, and it changed hands a few times before finally closing in 2011 after a 47-year run.

Damian's

For more than 40 years, Damian's Cucina Italiana at 3011 Smith Street was a premier destination for authentic Italian food in Houston. Founded by renowned restaurateur Damian Mandola, Damian's served upscale Northern Italian cuisine that made it a favorite for business or pleasure. Dishes like *linguine e gamberetti* with Gulf shrimp, veal piccata, breaded snapper, pork chop Milanese, fine steaks, and other traditional pastas and dishes put this place top of mind for many when it came to a nice dinner in Midtown. It even offered a shuttle to take diners to the theater district. But like a fine bottle of Barolo, nothing lasts forever. It held its final dinner service in August 2024. General Manager Johnny B. Mandola told the *Houston Chronicle*, "We never really recovered from the lockdowns." Inflation and flooding were also cited as factors.

ROTISSERIE FOR BEEF & BIRD

Joe Mannke's Rotisserie for Beef & Bird at 2200 Wilcrest was among the finest restaurants in town—some say the nation. Established in 1978, the restaurant had all but perfected steak, poultry, fish, and most notably, wild game. The Rotisserie for Beef & Bird had three private dining rooms: the wine cellar, the Heritage Room, and the library-like Hunt Room. A repeated recipient of *Wine Spectator's* Grand Award, the restaurant's wine cellar sported more than 19,000 bottles. After 25 years in business, the restaurant closed in 2004. Check out Mannke's book *Wanderlust: The Life of a Globetrotting Chef* for a glimpse into his flavorful life. Mannke's Bistro Le Cep restaurant at Wilcrest and Westheimer also went on to become a French-food favorite on the west side.

Great Caruso

In a world in which dinner patrons stare bleakly down at their iPhones so they can argue with strangers about politics, the concept of the old-school dinner theater is sliding into obscurity. But the Great Caruso carried the torch for many years. An intimate space ornate with a white marble staircase and a balcony box imported from an old European opera house, its patrons were treated to a rotation of singing talent and musical productions, all while awash in fine food and wine. What made it work was the quality of the performances; patrons saw a fantastic show up close. After a fire in 2006, however, the show did not go on. Let's hear a big round of applause for all the fun nights out the Great Caruso gave this city!

Maxim's

Sailing with Salvador Dali. Training at the New York World's Fair. Managing the Balinese Room. Camille Bermann's early life reads like a character from an Amor Towles novel. In 1949, he bought the Peacock Grill and renamed it Maxim's—Houston's first home of French haute cuisine. The restaurant offered a robust and sophisticated menu including *Pompano en Papillote*, poached trout Marguery, lobster thermidor, and caviar straight from the 21 Club in New York. Maxim's wine collection topped 70,000 bottles. The Schlumberger family guaranteed business among oilmen, who called Bermann "Frenchy," though he was actually from Luxembourg. Maxim's closed in 2001.

POULTRY

Fried chicken came to the region from other parts of the American South. Chickens were cheap and easy to prepare, and just about everyone kept them in their yard. So, when the fast-food craze hit Houston in the mid-20th century, we already had a yearning for yard bird. Bill Williams on South Main was one of the first popular fried chicken joints in town. Youngblood's was the next big bird brand, coming from Waco. And more recently, the Turkey Leg Hut put its unique spin on Ye Olde Drumstick. Sadly, though, all good wings must come to an end.

Courtesy of Pixabay

YOUNGBLOOD'S FRIED CHICKEN

Kids these days think they invented the side hustle. But during the Great Depression (1929–1939), most families needed an extra revenue stream to make ends meet. Speegleville cotton farmer Julius Youngblood raised chickens; he bought 500 chicks in 1930. To promote his business, he started Youngblood's Fried Chicken in Waco—boasting that they took chicken from farm to table. This idea is in vogue today, but back then it was way ahead of its time. People couldn't get enough. By 1967 the family had 30 locations, including one at 6441 South Main Street in Houston. In 1959 an ad for the Houston location promoted three big pieces of chicken, hot rolls and honey, a pickle slice, and your choice of fries or a baked potato—all for just 75 cents. But competition was intense, and the fast-growing company acquired too much debt. All the restaurants closed in 1969. There was a fun attempt to bring back the brand in Austin in 2017 using the original Youngblood family recipe, but this new venture flamed out at the end of 2018.

Bill Williams Chicken House

After a modest early effort made possible by a local oilman, Alabama native Bill Williams opened his first Bill Williams Chicken House at 6515 Main Street. The location was across the street from where Rice University played football prior to its on-campus stadium. His restaurant was a Rice Owl staple. Williams would eventually become known as "the Chicken King," opening additional restaurants in the area. His place out in Richmond, Texas, even had a motel! I mean, as far as motels go, having great fried chicken is as good a draw as anything. Williams also put his success to work for the community—donating big bucks to the Houston Livestock Show and Rodeo and its associated charities. The Bill Williams Chicken House on Main Street closed in 1973.

Courtesy of Boston Public Library

Photos courtesy of WPTDeepStacks

Turkey Leg Hut

Sometimes a concept just catches on fire, and Houston's Turkey Leg Hut (2015–2024) was a six-alarm inferno people couldn't get enough of. Originally a modest pop-up across from the Houston Livestock Show and Rodeo, Turkey Leg Hut served prehistoric-sized turkey legs that would put Ye Olde Renaissance Faire to shame. And—here's the fun part—they were smothered in all manner of deliciousness, like Cajun crawfish mac and cheese, Hennessey glaze, alfredo shrimp stuffing, and more. Seriously, these things looked like they could conceivably eat you first, and the place became a Houston destination with ridiculous lines. Turkey Leg Hut made owners Nakia Holmes and Lyndell Price local celebs. Eventually the place got messy with high-profile financial and legal problems, going out of business in December 2024. But it sure was good while it lasted.

BARS AND BREWERIES

Who wants a cold one? A lot of people here, as it turns out. From the old pre-Prohibition pioneers like the Houston Ice and Brewing Company and Gulf Brewing Company to modern open-late nightclubs, we've seen many beloved bars and breweries come and go. We've two-stepped at the Post Oak Ranch, Midnight Rodeo, and Blanco's. We've shaken our fists against the Man, and probably whoever stole your wheels, at Axiom. And we've played a quiet game of darts while watching Premier League Football at the Stag's Head, Ginger Man, and Richmond Arms. So let's raise a glass to Houston's many long-lost bars and breweries. Cheers to all the great nights, and a few fuzzy ones, that these places gave us.

Courtesy of HHRC

Houston Ice and Brewing Company

1890s Houston had no air conditioning; mud and horse poop stood in the streets; mosquitoes still spread diseases like yellow fever. But you know what? We had *amazing* beer. Local ice manufacturer and brewer Hugh Hamilton and his colleagues opened this massive brewing association on the banks of Buffalo Bayou, hiring German-born Fritz Kolb as the brewmaster. The business and its Magnolia Brewery produced award-winning brands including the hugely popular Southern Select. The business straddled the bayou with facilities on either side. It went flat, however, by 1950—the result of Prohibition, flooding, Hamilton's passing, and a bit of bad luck.

Courtesy of Texas Historical Commission

Gulf Brewing Company

Millionaire Howard Hughes (1905–1976) set flight records, made movies, worked with the CIA, and bought a Vegas hotel. He also produced the most popular Houston beer of his day. Hughes built the Gulf Brewing Company in 1933, just after Prohibition ended, on the grounds of the Hughes Tool Company at 5301 Polk Avenue. Its Grand Prize lager became a Texas favorite. By 1947, the brewery sold almost 483,000 barrels of beer annually. The enterprise failed in the 1960s, but in 2024 Saint Arnold Brewing Company revived Grand Prize beer for today's Houstonians.

Courtesy of Sam McCool

Midnight Rodeo

This popular honky-tonk opened in 1981 at Longpoint and Gessner but had many locations, including Katy. Execs could loosen their ties, hit the dance floor to two-step, listen to live music, and take the edge off the Houston heat with a few longnecks. In 1983, Midnight Rodeo rebranded as Wild West Bar. Willie Nelson, George Strait, Toby Keith, and other greats played the club. The dance hall eventually moved to 6101 Richmond Avenue in 1998, back when the Richmond Strip was hotter than a '90s Dodge Viper. The Midnight Rodeo survived Zima. It survived the Richmond Strip's decline. It even survived Billy Ray Cyrus's "Achy Breaky Heart." But it couldn't survive the government-mandated COVID-19 shutdowns, closing in 2020.

Courtesy of *This is Houston Magazine*

Dome Shadows

This popular nightclub opened in 1963 at 9218 Buffalo Speedway. It was located in a discreet shopping center just west of the Astrodome. Live music, a hot dance floor, and a laid-back attitude made this a very popular and progressive nightclub. This was back in the days of go-go dancers and those long, scary boots made for walkin'. Judge Roy Hofheinz was not happy about Dome Shadows using the name of his prized development. He sued owner Marshall M. Stewart for $1 million. Stewart counter-sued for his own million and won. While it opened as a swinging '60s kind of place, the club's format evolved. Reportedly the Ramones even played there in the 1980s. Today a condominium complex stands on the property.

Bayou Mama's Nightclub

The area around Richmond Avenue was the place to be seen in the 1990s. This included the popular Bayou Mama's nightclub at Gessner and Westheimer. I can almost hear "You Spin Me Round" and smell the fake smoke now. Some pretty popular performers made an appearance on the club's famous "Swamp Stage," and radio station 104 KRBE did live broadcasts that shared the club's popular music sets and hyped Bayou Mama's as a destination. You never knew who you'd run into. In 1991, Red Sox pitcher Roger Clemens was arrested at Bayou Mama's after getting into a fistfight.

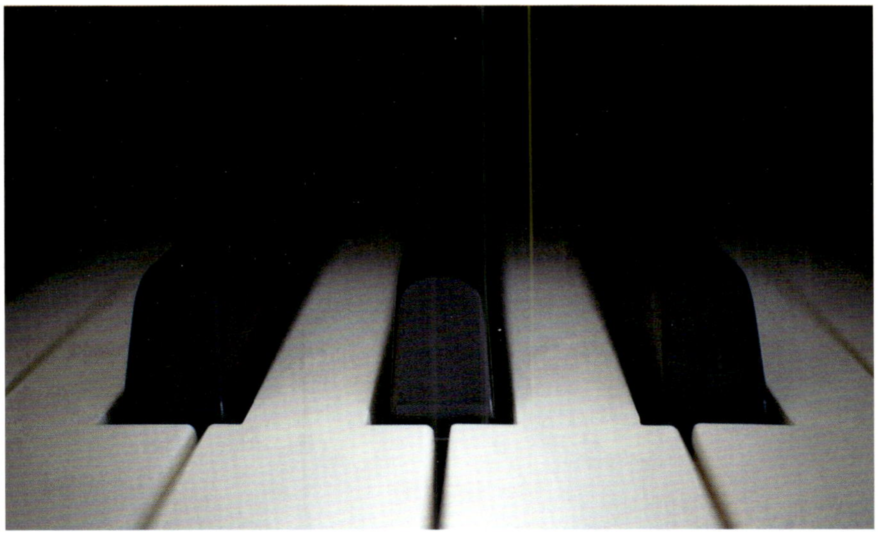

Courtesy of Johannes Plenio

City Streets

It's the 1990s in Houston. Can't decide whether to go two-stepping, visit a piano bar, or attend a rave? City Streets at 5078 Richmond had you covered. The club offered numerous nightlife experiences by walking from room to room. The club was built in The Windsor Shopping Center, which was originally home to the Windsor Cinerama Theatre—a luxury movie house that opened in 1962. The club rode the Richmond Strip's decline until last call in 2004. Today 5078 Richmond is a Golf Galaxy, which, given the age of former City Streets partygoers, might attract some of the exact same people.

Yucatan Liquor Stand

The Yucatan Liquor Stand at 6353 Richmond was a loud, high-energy dive bar back when the Richmond Strip was filled with young professionals blowing off steam from a long day at the office with far too many colorful drinks containing fruit. There was a sort of outdoor playground for grown-ups that was surprisingly large, complete with sand volleyball. They served perfectly acceptable bar food and crawfish when the season came around, and the place was downright riotous when people were into a big football, baseball, or basketball game. It was also an occasional concert venue; Kansas, Quiet Riot, and America all played the Yucatan Liquor Stand. While beloved in Houston back in the day, the beach/fishing/icehouse-themed bar was a franchise that could be found in many locations from London to Negril. According to the *Houston Chronicle*, in August 1992 the bar sold more drinks than any other club in town by volume.

Richmond Arms

A lively British pub and a personal favorite of mine for decades, the Richmond Arms at 5920 Richmond Avenue was owned by British entrepreneur Michael Holliday—who brought a number of popular enterprises to Houston. The parking lot of the Richmond Arms would be packed every Sunday morning as expats watched Manchester United, Arsenal, the Blackburn Rovers, Liverpool, and other teams in real time. There was a charming fireplace for winter months, a tremendous selection of fine beers, darts, good food, a generous patio, a popular quiz night, and always lively conversation to be had. While the sun finally set for the Richmond Arms empire in October 2023, a 40+ year run as a home-away-from-home for many is is something of which they should be proud.

The Black Labrador Pub

Courtesy of Michael Hart

The Black Lab served traditional British pub fare and a solid selection of fine beers for more than 30 years. The pub was at 4100 Montrose Boulevard. Parking was a little tight, but the business made up for it with authentic British comfort foods, great beer, a fun crowd, and a fantastic location. The oversized chess board out front on the bar's generous patio was always popular—though winning did get more difficult the longer you were there. People even brought their dogs. A jazz venue called Cezanne operated just upstairs from the pub. The nearby University of St. Thomas owned the building and entirely repurposed it for use by its students.

The Ginger Man

Named after the novel of the same name by J. P. Donleavy, which is a tragically fun read if you're a family man of about 30, the Ginger Man's cozy atmosphere and selection of imported beers made it hugely popular. Bob Precious opened the Ginger Man at 5607 Morningside in 1985—back when a watering hole for those who could appreciate a high-quality beer was still a novelty. It was smart but not stuffy with a cozy bar and plenty of outdoor tables. Precious grew the business to other markets, but the COVID-19 shutdowns killed the original in Rice Village. The good news: Next time you find yourself in the DFW area, you can still enjoy the Ginger Man's Irving, Texas, location.

Courtesy of Amy N.

Courtesy of Cottonbro Studio

Gallant Knight

Photos courtesy of David Greif

For 30+ years the house-turned-dive-bar at 2337 West Holcombe crammed R&B lovers to the rafters. Under a neon sign that let patrons navigate through the cigarette smoke, bands like Klockwork, Sammie Relford, and Hit Squad lit up the crowd. The party ended in 2006, until an entrepreneurial fan of the club reopened it in the summer of 2009 at 2511 Bissonnet. The new Gallant Knight worked hard to preserve the spirit of the original, even bringing in the former club's bartender. But a leasing dispute ended the Gallant Knight's new run for good at the end of 2010.

Kay's Lounge

Courtesy of Meredith Symonds

One of Houston's oldest bars when it closed, Kay's Lounge had a few different formats in the early days, including Kay's Barbecue and Kay's Club and Grill. It was started by the Edge family of Confederate House fame. The business had been in its current location at 2324 Bissonnet since 1944, a popular neighborhood bar known for its warm atmosphere, friendly staff, and big Texas-shaped table. Dr. Red Duke was a patron in his day, always appreciating that patrons gave him privacy on his off time. Eventually it was purchased by a real estate developer and razed on October 21, 2016—a very sad day indeed for Houston patrons. Sometimes the chemistry is just right to turn a place into a community, and that's the kind of happy hour alchemy that happened at Kay's Lounge.

Stag's Head

The Stag's Head at 2128 Portsmouth Street was another popular British pub owned by entrepreneur Michael Holliday. With 40+ beers on tap, a solid menu, and outdoor seating, it was a great place to gather with friends. The building had big windows, so it escaped the dark dinginess of some pub experiences (though I recognize sometimes that's what one wants). There were darts and sports on TV and arcade games and karaoke nights to pass the time, and it seems like someone was always holding a group event in the back room. But the good times came to an end in 2015 when the landlord decided not to renew the pub's lease.

Sherlock's Baker Street Pub

Opening in 1977, the game was afoot for 41 years at Sherlock's in the Carillon Center. My favorite thing about this place was its proximity to my house. But everyone could appreciate that it was both a cozy, quiet place to catch up with friends *and* a quite popular live music venue. It was also pretty big, with pool tables and a dance floor. St. Patrick's Day was packed and rowdy—in a good way. You could always catch a band with an Irish lilt like the Blaggards. New owners in 1995 grew the business, but the original at Westheimer and Briarpark closed in 2018. You can still deduce what it was like by visiting its Sugar Land location.

Courtesy of Edouard Dubiton

Scott Gertner's Skybar

Scott Gertner's Skybar was the place to be for R&B, jazz, and soul performances. The popular venue opened in 1999 on the top floor of a high-rise at 3400 Montrose Boulevard. For those who aren't aware, Gertner is a big deal: a talented three-time Grammy-nominated musician whose carefully curated musical acts added a personal touch to the place. When his original building aged out of service in 2010, the club moved into the Houston Pavilions, but the landlord eventually terminated its leasing agreement. Gertner came back with Scott Gertner's Sports Bar Live and Scott Gertner's Rhythm Room at 5535 Memorial Drive—a popular supper club with live music, dancing, and a contemporary Louisiana menu. Gertner passed away in May of 2025, having brought good times and great tunes to millions.

Blanco's Bar & Grill

The late Barry DeBakey, son of famed Houston surgeon Michael DeBakey, opened this popular and rustic Texas two-step joint. The sky-blue wooden building at 3406 West Alabama Street in River Oaks sported all kinds of Texas memorabilia, the full-body mount of a bison, and a small dance floor that never seemed to cool down. While music greats like Gary P. Nunn, Lyle Lovett, and countless others played there, it still had a quaint neighborhood feel. As a town, we "stopped loving her today" on November 30, 2013, when a nearby prep school bought the land Blanco's sat on.

Photos courtesy of Ron Hellman

Power Tools

This is where the cool kids partied between 1986 and the early 1990s. This exclusive and trendy dance club was housed in the old Magnolia Brewery building at 709 Franklin—the first real velvet rope "you're not on the list" experience in Houston. The original Power Tools was started in LA by Matt Dike, the co-founder of Delicious Vinyl records and one-time roommate of Jean-Michel Basquiat, and Jon Sidel. The two started Houston's sister club in 1986 and it absolutely set the Houston party scene on fire. When big-name celebrities played the stadiums, they came to Power Tools to party afterward. There were outrageous theme nights that included "Karma Sutra Slip 'n' Slide" and "Terrorism." There was an 18-foot Burmese python. There were dancers in chains. There was live music on the patio. It was too loud to talk. You communicated through dance and hand gestures and were glad to do it just to be part of the scene. The LA club closed in 1988. Houston's Power Tools changed ownership in 1991 before being unplugged for good in the mid-1990s.

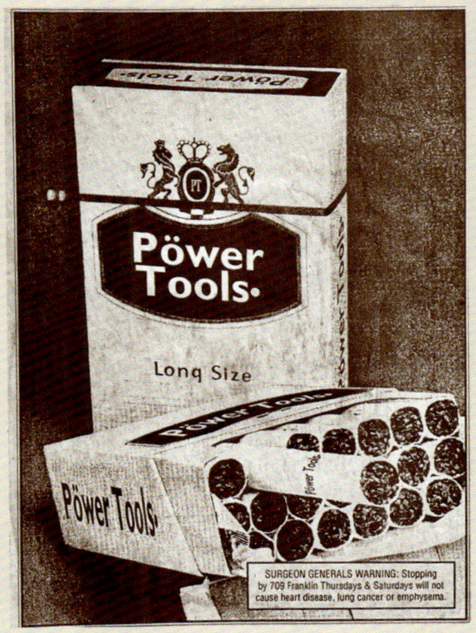

Post Oak Ranch

In Houston it's not unusual to see an architect or a dentist or an engineer drive an enormous Ford F-450 King Ranch super duty for no other reason than Texas. Back in the day, those folks partied at Post Oak Ranch. In the 1990s, this upscale honky-tonk was one of the hottest dance clubs in town. At 1625 West Loop South, the beauty of the Post Oak Ranch was location. You could be sitting at your corporate desk one minute, hit the Loop, exit, give your keys to the valet, and boom—"Lone Star" and "Cotton-Eyed Joe." The Post Oak Ranch was a fun intersection of city life and Texas two-stepping, complete with shot girls who wielded bottles of Jack Daniels and Jose Cuervo in leather holsters. It closed in the '90s, and today a La Quinta stands on the property.

ÉLAN

This private club was white-hot in the 1970s and 1980s. Many know this as the place where working class Bud (John Travolta) and fancy-pants Pam (Madolyn Smith Osborne) live it up during their dalliance in the 1980 film *Urban Cowboy*, though some insist that scene was shot at Cowboy on West Alabama. Regardless, élan was an enormous 17,000-square-foot elite party scene offering not just dancing but a library, several bars, and a nice restaurant. Eventually it became the Ocean Club, then came the Courtyard on St. James where we all went to luncheons and ate baked chicken. Today boutique office building 1885 St. James stands on the property.

STEAK HOUSES

While never a true Cowtown like Fort Worth or Abilene, Houston has always appreciated a good steak. Sonny Look of Look's Sir-Loin House and other restaurants brought Houstonians not only great steak but a love of fine wines. Bud Bigelow's gave us a charcoal-only experience. Houston's Trader Vic's offered not only a great steak but also a taste for Polynesian adventure. And the Old San Francisco Steakhouse was a swinging success for more than 35 years. Let's check on these rare Houston steak houses from the past and what they brought to the Bayou City.

Old San Francisco Steakhouse

Opening in 1973, the Old San Francisco Steakhouse at 8611 Westheimer Road was an 1890s-themed Old West–style restaurant inspired by the story of a romance between a Texas Ranger and a San Francisco woman. Patrons ate enormous steaks, fluffy baked potatoes, and other traditional steak house fare while a woman in period costume on a red velvet swing ventured high over the crowd. Meals always started with Swiss cheese and sourdough bread. Part of a San Antonio chain, Houston's Old San Francisco location was shut down in 2005 to make way for a new Target and associated strip center. This hardly seems like an upgrade.

Look's Sir-Loin House

Sonny Look's Sir-Loin House was an English Tudor Manor concept complete with exposed wood beams, a meat-tastic menu, and a mounted knight in armor out front. The first was in the Briargrove Shopping Center, though a South Main location came later. Four different flavors of butter were on each table. You'd often see proprietor Sonny Look, an influential and eccentric restaurateur who helped found the Conrad Hilton College of Hotel and Restaurant Management at the University of Houston, working the crowd in his trademark flamboyant jackets. The South Main location lasted the longest, finally closing in 1991 after Look suffered a stroke. Raise a glass to a true treasure of a Houston restaurateur.

Trader Vic's

Trader Vic's was the restaurant that helped bring "tiki culture" mainstream in the '50s and '60s. Glenn McCarthy's extravagant Shamrock Hotel at 6900 Holcombe was the perfect location for this Polynesian-themed restaurant and lounge here in Houston. People didn't come for the food; they came to imagine exotic and faraway shores and drink too many Polynesian-themed cocktails that were surely unsafe to smoke around. Houston's Trader Vic's location set sail for other shores in 1985 when the hotel's closing was imminent. But while Houston's best bet for a good mai tai these days is Lei Low in the Heights, Trader Vic's still has 25 locations in 11 countries if you're craving this singular steak experience.

Bud Bigelow's Charcoal House

Courtesy of HHRC

Opening in 1955 at 7939 Westheimer, Bud Bigelow's was arguably the hottest steak house in town for years. Practically in the suburbs when it opened, though in reality just between Gessner and South Voss, Houstonians came from all around for the restaurant's thick steaks, romaine salads, and other traditional steak house fare. The place was casual and also offered seafood, sandwiches, and hearty sides like potatoes au gratin and onion rings. Loaves of warm bread were brought to each and every table, gratis. The restaurant closed in 1982, and today that property is a storage facility with a total lack of charcoal awesomeness.

DINERS AND DRIVE-INS

A number of diners and drive-ins have come and gone over the years. Sadly, we don't have the space here to recognize them all. The Northeast is ground zero for classic roadside diners, but the popular restaurant style soon spread around the country. And as car culture changed America everywhere, Houston fell in love with the pull-up-and-eat experience. With 1950s decor, the 59 Diner was actually born in the 1980s. But a milkshake and fries felt like an authentic retro-themed experience. And while there was a small inside area, Montrose's Lucky Burger was a drive-in favorite. Roll down your window and let's order.

Courtesy of DL

59 Diner

The 59 Diner at 3801 Farnham was a late-night favorite for decades. Before new ownership rebranded it as the 59 Diner in the 1980s, it was actually called Phil's Restaurant. All the diner classics were available 24/7, from milkshakes, malts, and egg creams to burgers, omelets, chicken-fried steaks, and more. The 59 Diner may have been on an awkward island bordered by Farnham, Lexington, and South Sandman Streets, but its proximity to the freeway meant it was easy to reach, especially coming off of a late night (of work or play). The 59 Diner expanded to several locations, but the last three, including the original, shut in 2016 amid sudden financial hardship.

Courtesy of Michael Martin

Lucky Burger

This distinctive drive-in burger joint at 1601 Richmond in Montrose opened in 1975. It became a neighborhood fixture, selling cheap burgers to the eclectic residents of Montrose for decades. As the area gentrified, Lucky Burger seemed to exist in a time capsule. Why did the building have a strange barrel-like shape protruding from the rooftop? Glad you asked. The structure was originally an A&W Root Beer stand, so that big shape was made to resemble a giant root beer barrel that would draw in thirsty customers through the sheer gimmick of it. Which it did. Lucky Burger was eventually priced out of the space, and the neighborhood, closing in 2014.

Courtesy of John Margolies

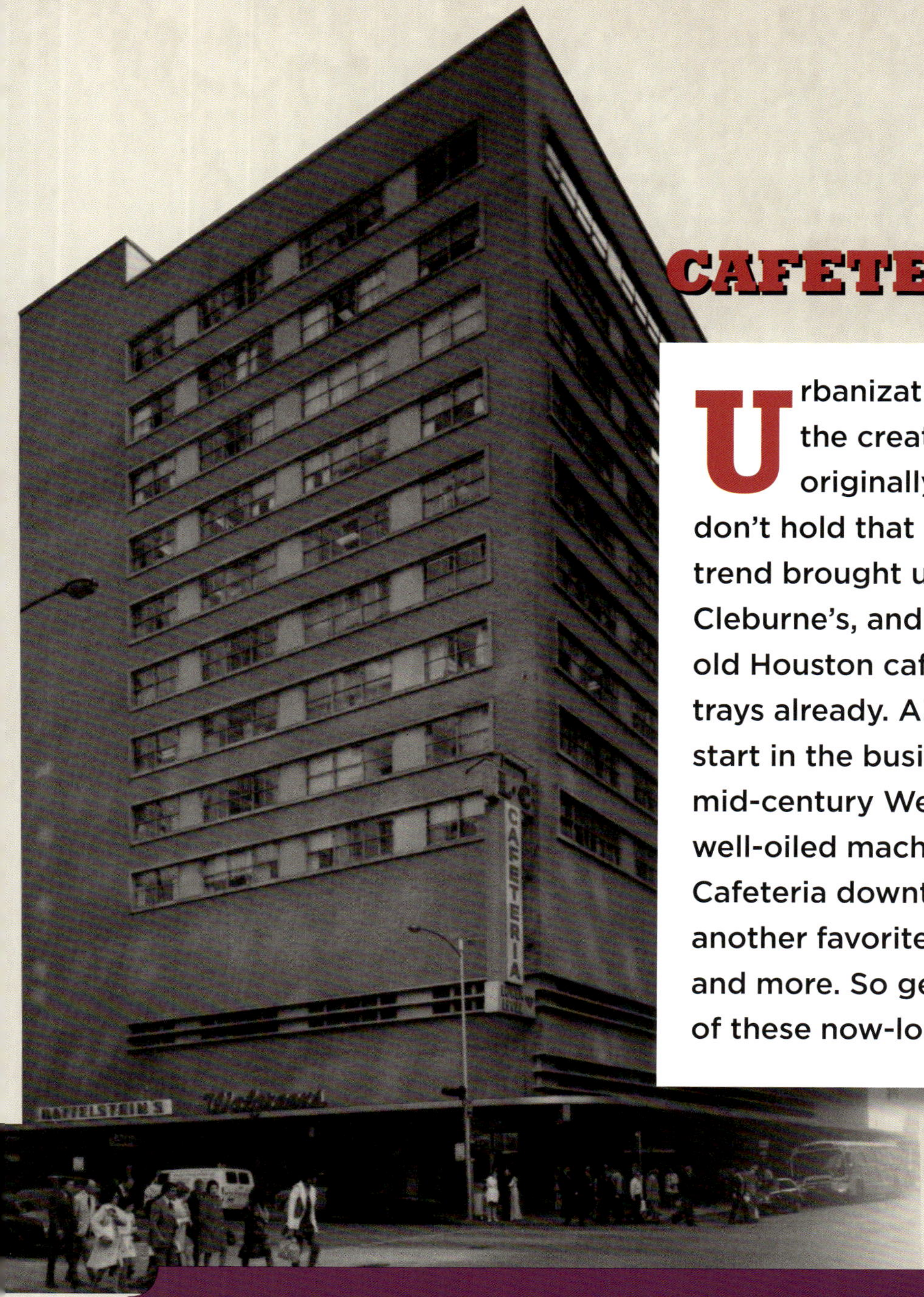

CAFETERIAS

Urbanization and industrialization drove the creation of the American cafeteria—originally in places like New York—but don't hold that against them. After all, that trend brought us places like Treebeard's, Cleburne's, and Luby's. Of course, some fine old Houston cafeterias have sadly put up their trays already. Allbritton's Cafeteria got an early start in the business and lasted decades. The mid-century Weldon Cafeteria was a sleek, well-oiled machine of a business. And the L-C Cafeteria downtown, and at other locations, was another favorite place for pot roast, potatoes, and more. So get in line as we recognize each of these now-lost Houston cafeterias.

Courtesy of HHRC

L-C Cafeteria

At 40,000 square feet, the L-C Cafeteria boasted that it was the largest cafeteria in the world. Opening in 1952 at 820 Main Street, the business had a 32-year run. The operation was so large it had its own butchers, bakers, laundry, and even machinists. There were four serving lines. You had to take the stairs or escalator down to the restaurant from street level, and rumor has it that the space was actually designed to be a bomb shelter. The business took its name from the surnames of the owners, John L. Lewis and Carr P. Collins. It closed in 1984 after selling the space to Walgreens.

Weldon Cafeteria

Popular as a family after-church spot, Weldon Cafeteria at 4916 Main Street was a big place—seating 600 people when it opened in 1949! Billing itself as "the South's newest and most modern two-line cafeteria," the building was groaning with classic Southern comfort fare such as chicken and dumplings, meatloaf, fried chicken, ham with red-eye gravy, mashed potatoes, collard greens, black-eyed peas, peach cobbler, and more. As remarkable as the food was its sleek mid-century building, which featured an "elevated sidewalk café" at which diners could eat outdoors but above street level. Weldon faded in the 1970s, but the building survives.

Courtesy of HHRC

Allbritton's Cafeteria

Luther L. Allbritton began selling fried fish, sandwiches, and other foods from his horse-drawn wagon in 1907. In 1915 he opened his first restaurant. By the time of his passing in 1949, Allbritton was able to hand down to his children a thriving cafeteria chain. Everything was made from scratch. They served home cooking like fried chicken, meatloaf, chicken and dumplings—more than 20 choices of meat with just about every traditional side or dessert you can imagine. They were also the first restaurant in town to list calories on the menu—an idea way ahead of its time. The last Allbritton's location closed in 1996, which is a pretty impressive run by any standard.

Courtesy of HHRC

PIZZA JOINTS

Pizza quietly snuck up on the South after WWII. One minute, nobody knew what it was, and the next thing you knew it was everyone's favorite food. Valian's Pizza on South Main was one of the earliest; many consider it Houston's original pizza. Kids packed the place after University of Houston football games let out. Over the years, Shakey's (part of a national chain), Barry's, and Big Humphry's became favorites. And of course downtown, Bombay Pizza grew a cult following with its subcontinental slices. Let's call up a few memories of piping hot pizza joints from Houston's past.

Courtesy of Ramon Velasquez via Wikimedia Commons

Bombay Pizza Company

Courtesy of April Vega

Bombay Pizza at 914 Main Street might not have been a longstanding Houston tradition, but it was a high-quality, groundbreaking restaurant that built a passionate following in its almost 13-year run. I loved this place. The concept was just as it sounds: fusion pizza with ingredients like saag paneer, chutney, masala, hummus, and more. Sides were above-average, with choices such as curried mashed potatoes and sauteed spinach. And the desserts like its *gulab jamun* and *ras malai* were top-notch. All with a long patio right off of the light rail line downtown. But, alas, the hardships imposed on small businesses in 2020 were the beginning of the end for this much-missed gem.

Barry's Pizza and Italian Diner

Barry's Pizza and Italian Diner at 6003 Richmond Avenue served fantastic pizza for 37 years. The distinctive building resembled a log cabin. Opening in 1983, Barry's was popular for its delicious deep-dish pizzas and impressive selection of beer. Owner Barry N. Childers was a hands-on leader, loved by customers and employees alike. Over the years, the business even grew to multiple locations. The 6003 Richmond Avenue building was in the heart of the Richmond Strip in its heyday, but business waned as the area cooled off as a popular night spot. The government shutdowns surrounding COVID-19 prompted its final *arrivederci* in 2020.

Courtesy of Sarah Pacilio

Big Humphrey's Pizza and Italian Restaurant

The late Jasper Vitale and his family ran this legendary Italian restaurant in Pearland—famous for authentic Sicilian dishes, great pizza, and fun twists on traditional favorites. Jasper's father, Joe Vitale, was a pro wrestler who opened his own restaurant in 1948 and worked there between matches. Cartoonist Ham Fisher actually based a character called Big Humphrey in his "Joe Palooka" comic strip on Joe Vitale. The name stuck. Originally on Park Place Boulevard, Jasper moved the restaurant to Pearland not long after his father's passing in 1977. After 34 years in the location, the business served its last slice in 2020.

Courtesy of Peter Bravo de los Rios

Shakey's Pizza

While Pizza Hut, Little Caesars, and Domino's got into the national pizza franchise scene early, Shakey's got there first. Started by Sherwood "Shakey" Johnson in 1954, this Sacramento, California–based pizza business paired great pizza with a Dixieland experience. Staff wore Kentucky Colonel ties and straw boater hats. There was plenty of cold beer, and someone in the place might even be playing a banjo now and again. Houston had numerous Shakey's locations at one time, including Bellaire Boulevard and Almeda Genoa Road. By the early 1980s, however, Shakey's had pulled out of Houston. But it's still a big deal for pizza-loving families in California and Washington state.

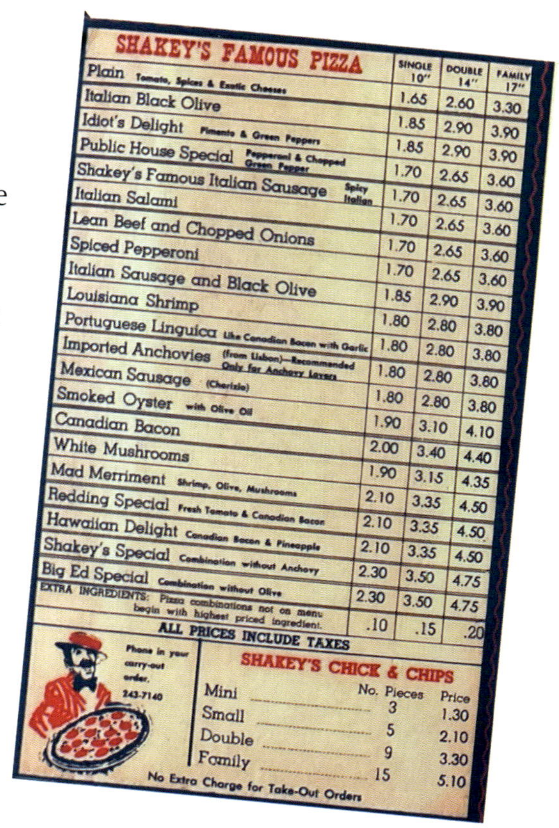

SHAKEY'S FAMOUS PIZZA	SINGLE 10"	DOUBLE 14"	FAMILY 17"
Plain Tomato, Spices & Exotic Cheeses	1.65	2.60	3.30
Italian Black Olive	1.85	2.90	3.90
Idiot's Delight Pimento & Green Peppers	1.85	2.90	3.90
Public House Special Pepperoni & Chopped Green Pepper	1.70	2.65	3.60
Shakey's Famous Italian Sausage Spicy Italian	1.70	2.65	3.60
Italian Salami	1.70	2.65	3.60
Lean Beef and Chopped Onions	1.70	2.65	3.60
Spiced Pepperoni	1.70	2.65	3.60
Italian Sausage and Black Olive	1.85	2.90	3.90
Louisiana Shrimp	1.80	2.80	3.80
Portuguese Linguica Like Canadian Bacon with Garlic	1.80	2.80	3.80
Imported Anchovies (from Lisbon)—Recommended Only for Anchovy Lovers	1.80	2.80	3.80
Mexican Sausage (Chorizio)	1.80	2.80	3.80
Smoked Oyster with Olive Oil	1.90	3.10	4.10
Canadian Bacon	2.00	3.40	4.40
White Mushrooms	1.90	3.15	4.35
Mad Merriment Shrimp, Olive, Mushrooms	2.10	3.35	4.50
Redding Special Fresh Tomato & Canadian Bacon	2.10	3.35	4.50
Hawaiian Delight Canadian Bacon & Pineapple	2.10	3.35	4.50
Shakey's Special Combination without Anchovy	2.30	3.50	4.75
Big Ed Special Combination without Olive	2.30	3.50	4.75
EXTRA INGREDIENTS: Pizza combinations not on menu begin with highest priced ingredient.	.10	.15	.20

ALL PRICES INCLUDE TAXES

Phone in your carry-out order. 243-7140

SHAKEY'S CHICK & CHIPS	No. Pieces	Price
Mini	3	1.30
Small	5	2.10
Double	9	3.30
Family	15	5.10

No Extra Charge for Take-Out Orders

Valian's Restaurant

"Pizza pie" was still a new and largely unknown concept in Houston in 1955 when George Valian opened Valian's Restaurant at 6935 South Main Street. Strategically located just across the street from the Shamrock Hotel, it wasn't his first restaurant—nor would it be his last. Armenian-born Valian took pizza big-time in Houston, eventually opening multiple Valian's Real Pizza locations as well as other beloved restaurant concepts. The Pappas brothers actually made Valian's pizza ovens. In its early days, a deluxe 12-inch pizza was just $2.25! While his restaurants sold other entrées, it was Valian's pizza that people all around town grew to crave. Valian's closed in the early '80s.

BAKERIES

Julia Child once said that a party without a cake is just a meeting. And with 24 Fortune 500 companies, Houston has enough meetings already. That's why we've always appreciated Houston bakeries, from the Acadian Bakery where you could always get a magnificent King Cake to André's Confiserie Suisse and its authentic European delights. Weingarten's started as a small bakery before eventually becoming a grocery empire. Here are a few samples of long-gone bakeries that have helped Houston celebrate everyday life.

Courtesy of Andre's Pastries

ANDRÉ'S
Confiserie Suisse

Courtesy of Andre's Pastries

André's was founded by Master Konditor-Confiseur André Bollier; the family still owns the business's flagship location in Kansas City. But Houston's location didn't feel like a franchise. André's was so utterly European, with its cozy wood, dainty quiches, and baroque little chairs. The food was flawlessly executed and authentic; the sweets and pastries were works of culinary art. It wasn't unusual to hear French or German being spoken in the place. You were almost shocked to find Houston's humidity and mosquitoes when you walked out the door rather than the honk of impatient taxis or the flutter of Paris pigeons. Today the original Houston location houses stylish Southern clothier Sid Mashburn. But the good news? Houstonians craving André's can still order online at andreschocolates.com and have their impeccable sweets shipped to Houston.

ACADIAN BAKERY

For more than 40 years, this Montrose bakery was your connection for an authentic King Cake. Sandy Bubbert bought the bakery at 604 West Alabama in 1979 from a pair of gentlemen who were moving back to Louisiana. They were kind enough to teach Bubbert all the tips and tricks on their way out of town. Bubbert went on to bake everyday goodies for the Montrose community, provide cakes for all kinds of delicious occasions, and even cater for noteworthy clients such as George H. W. Bush, Anne Rice, Shirley MacLaine, and Reba McEntire. The business closed in 2020, but we still savor the memories.

Courtesy of David Chien

ICE CREAM PARLORS

Houstonians don't sweat; they glisten. And since we've been known to glisten pretty hard even in fall and winter months, the ice cream business seems like a license to print money around here. Of course, ice cream parlors aren't just about the products—they're also about the people they bring together. Houston families, friends, first dates, and others have shared some wonderful ice cream parlor experiences in their day—from the old fashioned Rumpleheimer's, Swensen's, and Farrell's to the chic Neal's Italian Ice. So let's sit back and chill as we reminisce about the sweet memories of Houston's long-gone ice cream parlors.

Farrell's Ice Cream

This 1900s-themed restaurant out of Portland sported a menu seemingly concocted by out-of-control 8-year-olds who've somehow gained control of a business: ice creams, malts, banana splits, and the like. Houston had three locations: the Galleria, Northwest Mall, and Almeda Mall. The Galleria location was the one everyone seems to remember. Kids got a free sundae on their birthday. But the restaurant's coup de grâce was "Farrell's Zoo," consisting of 30 scoops of ice cream with marshmallow topping, bananas, sprinkles, whipped cream, cherries, and little toy animals. The Zoo was served on a stretcher carried by two people and accompanied by the sound of ambulance sirens. I love this country.

Swensen's

This popular San Francisco–based ice cream chain has helped keep America chill since 1948 and had numerous Houston locations back in the day, with stores at Hillcroft, Tanglewood, Woodlake Square, and way out west on Dairy Ashford. The first Swensen's had a repertoire of more than 150 flavors of fresh ice cream including some out-there ones like Swiss Orange Chip, which tasted like one of those chocolate oranges you get from Spec's. The delicious chain peaked here in the 1980s, and eventually all of its US stores closed. But you can still get this classic American ice cream experience overseas, ironically. So next time you're in Laos, Pakistan, or Malaysia, look them up.

Courtesy of David Disponett

Neal's Italian Ice

A lot of ice cream places Houston has seen over the years pretty much catered to kids and parents. After all, it takes a special kind of couple to share a banana split "trough" on a nice date night amid a phalanx of sugar-rushing 11-year-olds. But Neal's Italian Ice was an upscale place, perfect for an after-movie treat. Of course, kids loved it too. Italian ice is similar to sorbet, but more smooth and dense. It typically contains no dairy, though Neal's did have a white chocolate mousse flavor. Today Houston has at least seven specialty Italian ice shops, but sadly, Neal's is no longer one of them. But it was the trendsetter so many remember for bringing this delicious trend to the Bayou City.

Courtesy of Sandie Clarke

Rumpleheimer's Ice Cream

Courtesy of Rumpleheimer's

Located in the iconic Westbury Square, Rumpleheimer's was an 1890s-style restaurant and ice cream parlor sporting quaint little marble tables, old fashioned decor, and a coin-operated player piano. The staff even wore period dress. Rumpleheimer's offered a handful of ice cream and sherbet flavors, all kinds of specialty desserts, and waffles, as well as soups and sandwiches. They also sold old-fashioned rock candy on a stick by the cash register. Ads beckoned you to "return to yesteryear." It was a popular spot for families and young couples on a date, as well as a great way to wrap up a shopping trip around the square. Now this wonderful old place celebrating the bygone days has itself become a wonderful old memory of the past.

DELIS

Houston might be a long way from the old, original *Delikatessens* of Germany, but generations of both immigrants and lovers of fine food mean we've had some gouda ones. Well, far from the wurst, anyway. G. F. Sauter's brought deli food to Houston early in the 20th century. Alfred's carried the torch as a true Jewish deli for many years. We had the towering sammiches of Gugenheim's in the 1980s. And Leibman's served the Memorial area with distinction for decades. Take a number and lettuce remember some of the grand old delis from Houston's past.

Courtesy of HHRC

GUGENHEIM'S DELI

In the 1980s this New York-style delicatessen served up pastrami on rye, corned beef, Reubens, chicken soup, and potato knishes at the intersection of Post Oak and San Felipe. The restaurant was a partnership between a trio of businesspeople including Irvin Kaplan, one-time owner of the Houston Rockets. Some of the partners were already familiar with the delicatessen business, and others, such as entrepreneur Ghulam Bombaywala, conducted research by eating around the New York deli scene for a few days. A mid-1980s oil bust put the hurt on Houston's economy, and like many Houston businesses Gugenheim's would never see the 1990s.

Courtesy of Rachel Claire

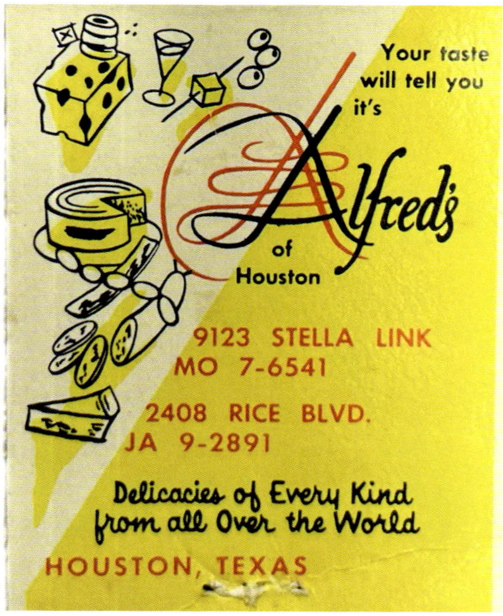

Alfred's of Houston

Alfred Kahn opened Alfred's of Houston in 1948 at 2408 Rice Boulevard. Khan was a German-American war veteran who'd escaped the Nazis in 1936. Alfred's was soon a local favorite. Its menu of home-cooked deli foods was extensive, serving up made-to-order corned beef hash, borscht, gefilte fish, lox, veal, and more. They even sold beer. It was a family place, but also the kind of restaurant at which a working man could get a steak at four in the morning. Kahn opened two more locations, but the business would fade in the mid-1990s following his passing.

Photos courtesy of Sharon Leibman

Leibman's
Wine & Fine Foods

I *loved* this place at 14529 Memorial Drive; everyone in our neighborhood did. It was a sit-down deli with a luxurious selection of fine cheeses, fresh-made breads and pastries, soups, side dishes, baked goods, chocolates, and more. Founders Ettienne and Ralph Leibman emigrated to Houston from South Africa, so there was no shortage of fine wines and even fun imported goodies. It was the perfect pre-dinner-party pit stop. After closing in 2017 when the couple retired, their family opened Leibman's Eatery at I-10 and Gessner, but the new place lost its lease in 2022 and closed. Here's to many great get-togethers that owed their success to Leibman's!

Cafe Sauter

This delicatessen and saloon opened at Travis Street and Preston Avenue in 1880. Houston's first restaurant to make use of electric fans, it was in business for 35 years. Founder Gustav F. Sauter was a Prussian who quickly built the eatery's reputation as a fine restaurant offering a robust menu full of European classics and local delicacies. One ad boasted the "finest imported and domestic table delicacies, wines, liquors, and mineral waters." Cafe Sauter was also apparently a pretty progressive place for its day, offering a "Ladies' Dining Parlor" upstairs. Today the old restaurant site is a parking lot.

{ENTERTAINMENT}

If you can't find something to do in Houston, you're just not trying. And it's almost always been that way.

Live music has always been part of Houston culture. Grassroots places like Liberty Hall and Fitzgerald's showcased a surprising amount of talent. And though progress has not been kind to Houston's country bar scene, the Redneck Country Club and Blanco's did us proud by bringing in many country music greats. Of course, Gilley's offered not just Friday Night Fist Fights, but also legendary music and dancing with a lively scene that went nationwide.

With weather like ours, it's always been "shut up and take my money" time for movie houses, live stage performances, and even drive-ins. Many were downright extravagant. The Metropolitan cost an astonishing $2 million to build in 1926. That's about $35 million in today's money!

Whenever I mentioned this book project, AstroWorld came up, of course. No, not the Travis Scott album—actual AstroWorld. Houstonians rode roller coasters, played games, splashed around, and even attended shows at the beloved park. Its closure broke our hearts. The 340-foot Astroneedle was supposed to be shipped down to Mexico after AstroWorld's closure but was eventually scrapped along with most of the rides and attractions.

Houston golfers are basically survivalists, though not all of our courses have made it over the years. Players at yesterday's courses, like Bear Creek Golf World, managed their approach shots among alligators and Amazon-esque numbers of mosquitoes.

Then there were the sports venues, which grew with the city and hosted both championships and broken hearts. I find Compaq Center among the most interesting, transitioning from hosting the Houston Rockets and arena football games to Joel and Victoria Osteen's popular Lakewood Church.

Let's throw on a t-shirt and see how past Houstonians had fun.

AstroWorld Dolphin Show
Courtesy of HHRC

Leon Beck at Gilley's
Courtesy of Leon Beck

Ted Nugent
Courtesy of Republic Country Club

Airline Drive-In Screen
Courtesy of HHRC

Colt .45 Game
Courtesy of HHRC

Courtesy of HHRC

AMUSEMENT PARKS

Many Houston rides have slowed and stopped forever. Of course, AstroWorld is top-of-mind for everyone. And to think they never really did much with the land. Pity that. But there were also places for the wee tikes, like Peppermint Park. The OG place in town was Luna Park, quite a novelty in its day. Houston's Busch Gardens was really fun but evaporated faster than a case of beer at a frat party. And places like Malibu Grand Prix and Celebration Station let Gen Xers like me live it up without getting into too much trouble, with a few tragic exceptions. Let's buy some game tokens and visit the amusement parks of Houston's past.

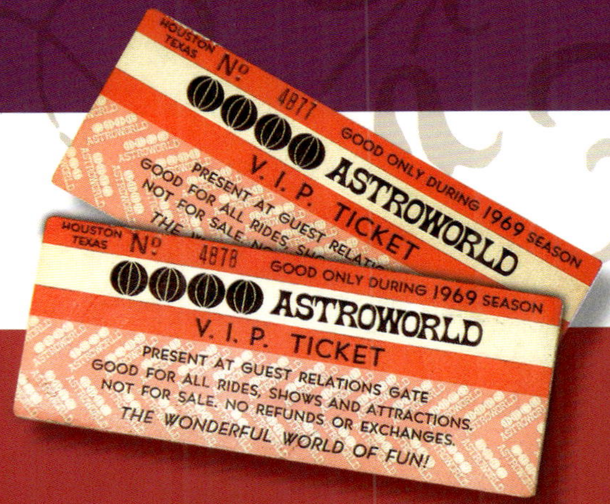

Courtesy of Cristan Williams

AstroWorld

Opened in 1968, AstroWorld was part of Roy Hofheinz's "Astrodomain" complex that included this theme park, the Astrodome, a hotel, and other facilities. The park offered roller coasters and other high-speed rides, shows, restaurants, and themed areas like Western Junction, Plaza de Fiesta, and the European Village. Six Flags bought the park in 1975, and WaterWorld was added in 1983. The park had a huge outdoor cooling system so visitors could stay chill in the dead heat of a Texas summer. AstroWorld was closed in 2005, and today the land is mostly used for Houston Livestock Show and Rodeo overflow parking.

Busch Gardens

Beer magnate Adolphus Busch (1839-1913) started Busch Gardens as a way to sell and promote his beer. It worked. As the concept scaled nationwide, each park had a different theme to distinguish itself. Houston's location opened Memorial Day of 1971 with a Far East theme. It sported distinctive Asian pagodas and wild exotic animals, including polar bears. The park was right by the brewery at 775 Gellhorn Drive. But there were only so many amusement park dollars to go around town, and it couldn't compete with AstroWorld. Houston's Busch Gardens closed in 1973, but the locations in Tampa, Florida, and Williamsburg, Virginia, are still going strong.

Courtesy of HHRC

Luna Park

Luna Park opened in the summer of 1924 near Woodland Heights, billing itself as "the Coney Island of Texas." The park bragged that its Giant Skyrocket roller coaster was "the world's most thrilling roller coaster." I'd argue it's hard to quantify thrillingness, but it was Houston's first roller coaster regardless. The park had rides, games, and big events like beauty and dancing contests. Things went downhill in the late '20s as the stock market crashed and Houstonians were more worried about shooting dinner than shooting for stuffed animals. Crime worsened, and the fun ended for good in 1934. This is why we can't have nice things down here.

Malibu Grand Prix
Family Entertainment Center

Before home video games, the internet, and streaming media, kids went places for fun. Out in the actual world. And in Carter/Reagan/Bush-era Houston, that place was often Malibu Grand Prix. Here kids could drive little gas-powered race cars, play arcade games, duke it out at mini golf, ride bumper boats, and swing for the fences in a batting cage. Houston had two long-standing Malibu locations, one off the West Loop and another off the Southwest Freeway. For no reason other than it was cool, the West Loop location had an arcade resembling a castle. But the wheels fell off in the 1990s.

Peppermint Park

This small, family-owned amusement park chain was designed just for young children and operated parks in a few different cities. The Houston location opened its no-doubt sticky doors in the 1950s, actually getting its start in the parking lot of a Sears in Pasa-get-down-dena. Eventually it moved and upgraded to a red-and-white building so all that coastal rain wouldn't ruin the fun. Rides included everything young kids like, such as bumper cars, merry-go-rounds, little Model T cars, a "whip ride," swing rides, a Ferris wheel, and much more. But everything at Peppermint Park came to a stop in 1989.

Courtesy of Amanda Pape

Courtesy of Panaromio

Celebration Station

Many Houstonians my age have fond memories of Celebration Station's go-karts, video games, bumper boats, and birthday parties. This hot spot for family fun had two Houston locations. The first was at 6767 Southwest Freeway, which opened in 1991. This was peak arcade time for Street Fighter II (I always played Dhalsim). A second location at 180 Rankin Road opened the same year. This is actually a franchise that's still thriving today in other cities. But the Southwest Freeway location became a Zuma Fun Center in 2005, and both of Houston's Celebration Station facilities have now been demolished.

LIVE THEATER

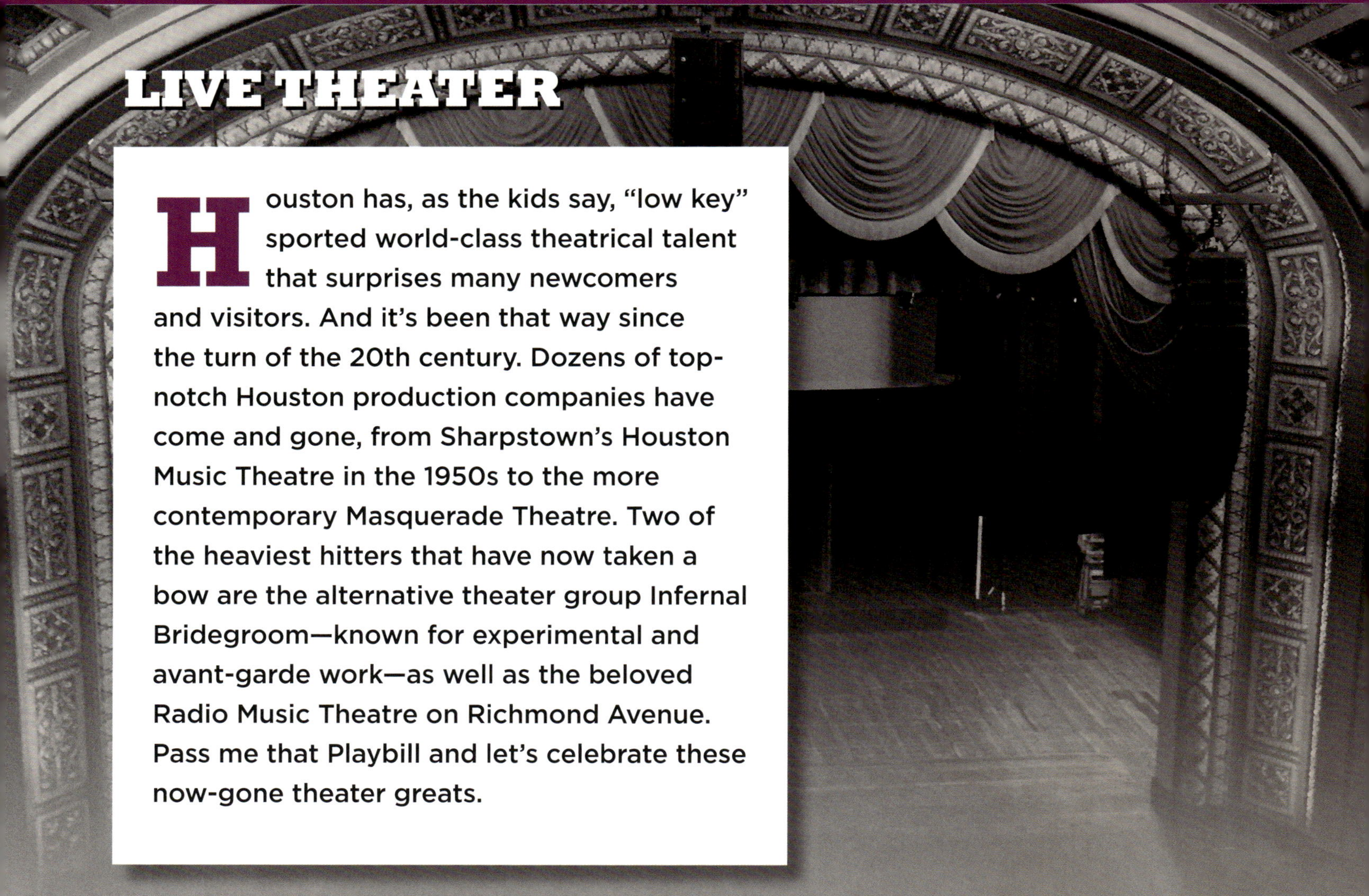

Houston has, as the kids say, "low key" sported world-class theatrical talent that surprises many newcomers and visitors. And it's been that way since the turn of the 20th century. Dozens of top-notch Houston production companies have come and gone, from Sharpstown's Houston Music Theatre in the 1950s to the more contemporary Masquerade Theatre. Two of the heaviest hitters that have now taken a bow are the alternative theater group Infernal Bridegroom—known for experimental and avant-garde work—as well as the beloved Radio Music Theatre on Richmond Avenue. Pass me that Playbill and let's celebrate these now-gone theater greats.

Usflibstudent21 via Wikimedia Commons
https://creativecommons.org/licenses/by-sa/4.0/deed.en

Radio Music Theatre

RMT is a treasure missed by so many Houstonians, me included. This intimate live theater venue at 2623 Colquitt Street opened in 1985. Founded by Steve and Vicki Farrell, two great comedic talents, RMT performed original homespun musical comedies with quirky characters and lots of tongue-in-cheek satire. Many of the shows featured recurring settings and characters, such as the hilariously dysfunctional small-town Texas Fertle family. Their end-of-year show, *A Fertle Holiday*, was always a hit. It was, in fact, as cute as a little baby owl. The quality of the writing, production, and performances made RMT something special for Houstonians until its 2014 closing.

Courtesy of Historic Images Entertainment 3

Infernal Bridegroom Productions

Every big city has a berserker avant-garde theater company running around thrilling audiences and terrifying the mainstream theater establishment. Between 1993 and 2007, this was Infernal Bridegroom Productions. Founded by Jason Nodler, Jim Parsons, Tamarie Cooper, and other prominent names, the company produced 68 thought-provoking works: a mix of edgy classics and originals. Their shows were sometimes performed in unconventional spaces—including, once, a moving bus. Later performances were held at the Axiom, an alternative and punk rock music club. Today many of IBP's players can be found at Nodler and Cooper's the Catastrophic Theatre at MATCH, where the team once again pushes the envelope for contemporary theater.

Courtesy of Birmingham Museums Trust

The Comedy Workshop

Opening in 1978, the Comedy Workshop and its Comix Annex was a popular showcase for national-level comedic talent. The Farrells of Radio Music Theatre fame, along with Paul and Sharon Menzel, concepted the club at the southwest corner of San Felipe and South Shepherd. The venue, which was wildly popular from the jump, gave rise to a group of influential entertainers known as the Texas Outlaw Comics—though they weren't all strictly from here. These included Bill Hicks (who is 100 percent not Alex Jones), Sam Kinison in his prime years, Andy Huggins, Steve Epstein, Ron Shock, Jimmy Pineapple, Dee Macaluso, John Farnetti, Riley Barber, and Carl LaBove. Actress, writer, and stand-up comedienne Brett Butler, of Grace Under Fire fame, performed there. Countless people who came up through the Comedy Workshop went on to bring the world amazing talent, and it served as a real cultural center of gravity before closing in the early 1990s. Today the building is a Spec's.

Courtesy of Bogomil Mihaylov

DRIVE-IN MOVIE THEATERS

There are things that are more American than a date at a drive-in movie, but not many things. And Houston has had its share of great drive-ins from the boom of the 1950s and 1960s to the retro rebirth. Houston has had dozens: the old Post Oak, the Shepherd, the McLendon Triple, the old Loew's Sharpstown and Airline to name a few. Shhhhh . . . the sound is on. Let's screen some long-gone H-Town drive-ins.

Courtesy of HHRC

Loew's Sharpstown Open-Air Theatre

Standing on 36 acres, the Loew's Sharpstown at 6366 Bellaire Boulevard held from 1,200 to 1,700 vehicles. That's more than 4,000 people if you count the people in the trunk! (Kidding.) But that's massive. The theater cost more than a million bucks to build, and that's late 1950s dollars, mind you. It opened in 1958 sporting a miniature train, an enormous cafeteria, and even a petting zoo that included, bless its poor heart, an actual black bear that drank Coca-Cola. Alas the Cycle of Retail Entropy spares few, and after a humiliating decline the Loew's Sharpstown would tank in 1976.

Courtesy of Cinema Treasures

The Shepherd Drive-In

The Shepherd opened at 6004 North Shepherd on May 23, 1947. *Rage in Heaven* with Ingrid Bergman and Robert Montgomery played at the theater's opening night. Early Houston drive-in entrepreneurs Claude Ezell and W. G. Underwood, who owned theaters all around Texas, were the driving force behind the business. The Shepherd was designed by architect Jack Corgan who, while specializing in theaters, also designed the terminal at Dallas Love Field. Today the patch of land on which the Shepherd once stood is the location of a Reddy Ice facility, for which we are always appreciative here in the steamy South.

Photos courtesy of Cinema Treasures

THE POST OAK DRIVE-IN

The Post Oak opened on March 14, 1951, at 2900 South Post Oak Boulevard. The vision of a gentleman named Jack Groves Sr., the theater had the capacity for more than 600 cars! When the land was sold in 1960, the entire theater was taken apart and re-assembled at 1255 North Post Oak Road between the Katy Freeway and the Hempstead Highway. One of the most popular and quirky attractions at the Post Oak was a taxidermied moose that Groves himself had shot. Affixed with a radio, the moose would make announcements and even talk to kids on occasion.

Photos courtesy of Cinema Treasures

Courtesy of Library of Congress

Courtesy of Cinema Treasures

The Airline Drive-In

Another of Claude Ezell's ventures, the Airline Drive-In at 4507 Airline Drive opened on June 10, 1950. Its premier movie was the Randolph Scott western *Canadian Pacific*—which must have been great on the big screen with its sprawling mountain vistas from Banff and the like. The theater took up 12 whole acres and included a snack bar with car service, as well as a playground with an attendant. The theater, with its neon lights and iconic airplane on the screen tower, had real staying power over the years. Willie Nelson actually gave a concert there in 1978, though the theater finally closed in the early 1980s.

Courtesy of HHRC

Courtesy of Cinema Treasures

The McLendon 3

Gordon Barton McLendon was a DFW-based Yale graduate, filmmaker, author, and media mogul. His McLendon 3 drive-in opened May 7, 1971, at 11991 South Main Street—a novelty because of its three screen towers. Opening night was a fondue buffet of cheesy drive-in fare that included *One More Train to Rob* and other films. George Peppard himself was on hand to celebrate the theater's opening. McLendon stood out because not only did he own drive-in theaters, but he also vertically integrated—producing movies like the riotously low-budget 1959 film *The Killer Shrews*, which I've somehow managed to see about five times (spoiler: the shrews appear to be coon hounds). The McLendon shut down in 1986 to make way for a flea market. Today the property is an RV park.

Courtesy of Cinema Treasures

MOVIE THEATERS

These days Houstonians take for granted being able to throw on some athleisure wear and catch a movie at their neighborhood theater. That's if you can be bothered to not just watch live premiers on your iPad at home. Back in the day, however, going to the cinema was an event. Many of the long-lost cinemas of Houston were astonishingly lavish, and a place to be seen. Looking sharp was a must. Check out the book *Cinema Houston: From Nickelodeon to Megaplex* by David Welling and Jack Valenti for a more detailed look at the grand old long-gone Houston movie houses.

Courtesy of The Beaty Mercantile

The Isis Theatre

This 900-person silent film theater had a plush Egyptian theme, an exquisite 20-foot-high organ, and an advanced air circulation system that involved blowing air past actual blocks of ice—which must have felt heavenly in August. The Metropolitan years later would one-up the Isis on the luxury Egyptian front, and swanky theaters soon proliferated. The Isis closed in the late 1920s. After lying vacant, part of the building became the Mercury Room, also now closed. Today the basement is Underground Hall; the handrail leading down was salvaged from the old theater.

Courtesy of HHRC

Landmark Greenway

Located in Greenway Plaza, the Greenway 3 Theatres opened in 1974. After being just another first-run mainstream theater, the Greenway began specializing in art house and independent films. My wife and I saw Morgan Spurlock's *Super Size Me* there. When the film mentioned Houston as the nation's fattest city, the crowd erupted. Weird flex, but I guess we'll take what we can get down here. (That movie came out in 2004. As of this writing, McAllen, Texas, down in the Valley has that honor.) The Greenway closed in 2007.

Photos courtesy of Cinema Treasures

Majestic Theatre

Courtesy of HHRC

Completed in 1910, the Majestic at the 800 block of Texas Avenue was built with intricate tile, marblework, plate glass, and textiles with European-inspired designs. The Majestic was a vaudeville theater, not a movie house. Vaudeville, which sounds tremendously antiquated these days, meant rather than one long show, audiences got several smaller acts. You might see a violinist, a circus act, a magician, or a singer. That way chances are you saw something you really enjoyed, and there was always a variety. The 1910 Majestic was actually one of three Houston Majestic locations over the years. The Majestic at 800 Texas was renamed the Palace Theatre in 1923, which closed in 1946. The space eventually became a part of the *Houston Chronicle*'s downtown offices until the building's eventual demolition in 2016. The Texas Tower stands on the space today.

Courtesy of HHRC

Loew's State Theatre

Alfred C. Finn, designer of the San Jacinto Monument, served as the architect for the Loew's State Theatre at 1022 Main Street. Opened in 1927 to much fanfare, the interior was a monument in itself, with massive marble-floored lobbies, bronze doors, elaborate textiles, and decorations that included actual European antiques. Apparently one of the Vanderbilts had liquidated a Manhattan townhouse, and the theater took the opportunity to pick up a number of historic French antiques and *objets d'art.* People came to see the theater itself as much as they did the shows, which included silent films, live performances, and contemporary "talkies" over the years. It was demolished in 1973.

The Metropolitan Theatre

Courtesy of HHRC

The $2 million Metropolitan Theatre at 1016 Main Street took the luxury Egyptian theme to a new level in a way the old Isis could not. The discovery of King Tutankhamun's tomb in 1922 had brought the mysteries of ancient Egypt into global popular culture, and when the Metropolitan opened on Christmas Day of 1926 the line was around the block. You got dressed up for the Metropolitan. A full orchestra accompanied stage performances, and the screen showcased some of the world's greatest works of film during the Metropolitan's 40+ years of operation. The luxurious old theater was demolished in 1973.

Alabama Theatre

The Alabama Theatre at 2922 South Shepherd Drive opened in 1939, one of Houston's most beloved bits of art deco architecture. The Alabama hosted both live performances and cinema over the years, but its run came to an end in 1983. The building eventually fell vacant. In 2006, the old Alabama reopened as a Bookstop, and today it serves as a Trader Joe's. So while the building is still there, its transition from charming local movie house to seller of Organic Elote Corn Chip Dippers for a German supermarket conglomerate makes it seem like a lost treasure to me.

NIGHTCLUBS AND MUSIC VENUES

Saloons and dance halls were some of the first buildings to go up in Houston. It's as though the city founders looked around and said, "Well, if we're going to live here, we'll need a place to drink excessively while listening to music." Here's to many great music memories yesterday's clubs have provided, from the hippie days of the Sand Mountain Coffee House to Skynyrd at Liberty Hall, the old Satellite Lounge, and Stafford's Redneck Country Club. I was tempted to include Rockefeller's but didn't. I mean, you can still see a concert there. It would be like that Monty Python plague skit where they keep trying to put the live guy into the cart. And, of course, if you haven't paid homage to Gilley's lately it might be time to watch *Urban Cowboy* again. Hey, the opening act is walking onto the stage; let's do this.

Courtesy of Dave Meeks

The Redneck Country Club

Courtesy of Redneck Country Club

For live music and laid-back Southern charm, the Redneck Country Club couldn't be beat. Concepted by radio celebrity Michael Berry at 11110 West Airport Boulevard in Stafford, the RCC featured legendary country performers and an old-school atmosphere promoting respect for veterans, American values, and Texas pride. Music greats Charley Pride, Merle Haggard, the Bellamy Brothers, the Oak Ridge Boys, Ray Wylie Hubbard, Willie Nelson, and many more played the RCC. Touches like lawn chairs, kitschy trailer decor, and an actual General Lee Dodge Charger along with homegrown events like armadillo races made it a genuine Houston treasure. The club eventually rebranded as Republic Country Club & BBQ but closed permanently in March of 2020 as a result of the government shutdowns during the COVID-19 pandemic.

Courtesy of Vitalii Khodzinskyi

Fabulous Satellite Lounge

Owned by Houston musician, producer, and entrepreneur Dickie Malone, the Fabulous Satellite Lounge at 3616 Washington opened in 1992. This popular music venue hosted some of the biggest alternative acts of the 1990s. One of the best things about the place was that it wasn't a big, soulless warehouse; it booked awesome talent but was still intimate enough that you felt connected to the performers. I remember seeing the Old 97's at the Satellite in about 2001, and I'm pretty sure the Gourds opened for them playing bluegrass covers of West Coast gangster rap. Of course, drink had been taken, so I could be mistaken. But the place was laid back, and the bookings top-notch. Sadly, the club closed in 2002 when the landlord refused to renew its lease.

The Axiom

Courtesy of JR Delgado

Oi! If you liked loud, irreverent music in the late 1980s and early 1990s, ever owned a spiked wristband, or drew "anarchy" symbols on your skateboard—you probably partied at the Axiom. The building at 2524 McKinney Street was once a small hotel, before J. R. Delgado made it ground zero for Houston's edgy party scene. The neighborhood was sketchy, but the crowd was cool. Big name bands like Nirvana, GWAR, Youth of Today, Fugazi, the Dead Milkmen, Melvins, Flaming Lips, Yo La Tengo, and countless more played the club. It also showcased a lot of local talent through bands like Sugar Shack, Pain Teens, Verbal Abuse, and others. It was about more than the shows; it was a scene and a community remembered fondly by many. No word on how many former patrons now drive Volvos and listen to NPR.

Courtesy of JR Delgado and Kevin Bakos

Courtesy of Michael Hart

Courtesy of Elephante Blanco

Fitzgerald's

The building at 2706 White Oak Drive was a Polish dance hall before it became Fitzgerald's in 1977. Sara Fitzgerald owned the club for more than 40 years, during which time it became one of the most popular and beloved concert spots in all of Texas. Intimate and a little rustic, Fitzgerald's brought Houstonians absolute on-fire shows by ZZ Top, James Brown, the Red Hot Chili Peppers, Joe Ely, American Aquarium, Stevie Ray Vaughan, the Ramones, David Allan Coe, and countless others. Generations of Houstonians have fond memories of Fitz's. But while the "road goes on forever and the party never ends," Fitzgerald's final show was held at the end of 2018.

Walter's on Washington

At 4215 Washington Avenue, Walter's made a big impact on Houston music. Started by Pam Robinson in 2000, the venue hosted a diverse mélange of independent artists. It felt less hardcore than the Axiom, maybe just because of the neighborhood, though likely your parents still probably had never heard of any of the artists. Still, I saw a Weezer tribute band there once, so it wasn't that hardcore. In 2012, Walter's on Washington reinvented itself as Walter's Downtown at 1120 Naylor Street. Robinson passed away in 2014, and her son, Zack Palmer, continued the family business until its closing in 2018. The venue may be gone, but the memories of so many high-energy shows still reverberate all around town.

Liberty Hall

This was a legendary music venue in its day. At 1610 Chenevert Street, it brought some of the hottest musical acts of the 1970s. Opening in 1971, the club's original owners were Ryan Trimble, Michael Condray, and Lynda Herrera, who brought in an arsenal of talent including Lynyrd Skynyrd, Townes Van Zandt, ZZ Top, Waylon Jennings, Clifton Chenier, Johnny Winter, Ted Nugent, and more. They also had some fantastically designed concert posters, I have to say. But that's a tough business, and the club closed in 1978 due to a number of factors including financial challenges and a changing music scene.

Sand Mountain Coffee House

Courtesy of Jefferson Santos

At one time, Sand Mountain Coffee House was Houston's premier live folk music venue, occupying a house that used to be a dance studio at 1213 Richmond Avenue. Sand Mountain brought in crazy talent like Guy Clark, Jerry Jeff Walker, Lightnin' Hopkins, Janis Joplin, Vince Bell, and more. The club's founders were still in high school and had to get parental help with all the business's administrative functions. They named it after founder John Carrick's favorite song at the time, the harmonica-laden "Sand Mountain Blues" by the Delmore Brothers. By the end of 1976, the business had run its course.

Gilley's in Pasadena

Talk about a Southeast Texas legacy! Popular with plant folk in the area, Gilley's in Pasadena (1970) was listed by the *Guinness Book of World Records* as the world's largest honky-tonk. Willie Nelson, George Jones, Merle Haggard, Alabama, Charlie Daniels, Loretta Lynn, and other big-name country stars all played Gilley's. The club had a mechanical bull, punching bags, showers for truckers, and a dance floor so big it practically had its own weather patterns. If you haven't seen *Urban Cowboy*, close this book and go stream it now. Gilley's burned in 1990 after the partners had a falling out. But locations in Dallas and Vegas arose from the ashes to two-step onward.

SPORTS VENUES

There's something not just cultural but maybe even tribal about the places where we cheer on the home team. Houston came together as a community at Buffalo Stadium, Colt Stadium, and the Astrodome for America's greatest pastime. The crowd at the Astrodome also went wild for the Houston Oilers back in its day. And we even rooted for Houston animals at the Epsom Downs horse races, the Houston Livestock Show and Rodeo's time at Sam Houston Hall, and the big dogs of Gulf Greyhound Park. So please rise as we recognize Houston's bygone sports venues.

Courtesy of Library of Congress

Gulf Greyhound Park

When this massive La Marque dog track opened in 1992, it was the largest greyhound racing facility in the world. An average of around 5,000 people attended each race at Gulf Greyhound Park in the track's opening year. Greyhounds can run up to 45 miles per hour, and the crowd went crazy betting on the dogs and watching them race. The facility had a clubhouse, food, beer, and simulcast racing, all in a family-friendly environment. And it was a cheap, fun way to kill a nice afternoon with friends. When the track closed in the summer of 2020, it ended live dog racing in Texas.

Epsom Downs

Before the city had Sam Houston Race Park, it had Epsom Downs near the intersection of Jensen Drive and the Eastex Freeway. When Texas approved pari-mutuel betting in 1933, Epsom Downs was the first horse track built in the state (though not the last). Named after a famous horse track in England, almost 30,000 people came to see the first race. The track had enough horse stalls to accommodate 800 animals. In 1937, the governorship changed hands, and pari-mutuel betting was once again outlawed in Texas—ending the fun at Epsom Downs and other tracks across the state.

Courtesy of HHRC

Buffalo Stadium

Before we had the Astros, or even the Colt .45s, we had the Buffaloes. This minor league baseball team played for a respectable 65 years between 1896 and 1961. And Buffalo Stadium was their home. The team played in what was called the Texas League. The stadium was on the southeast side, roughly across Interstate 45 from the University of Houston and bracketed by Cullen Boulevard, Leeland Street, Coyle Street, and Milby Street. Opening day at Buffalo Stadium was April 11, 1928. It was later renamed Busch Stadium, and it hosted its final game in 1961.

Courtesy of HHRC

Sam Houston Hall

Sam Houston Hall was built for the 1928 Democratic Convention. Houston was not an obvious choice to host this event in the heat of summer, and there was a bit of Southern political stigma in the years following the War Between the States. This was the first Democratic Convention held in the South after the war, essentially because Jesse H. Jones was the Democratic National Committee's director of finance. The building seated 20,000 people. Once the convention was over, it housed the Houston Livestock Show and Rodeo between 1932 and 1936—after which it was demolished. Today that site is the Hobby Center for the Performing Arts.

Courtesy of Library of Congress

Courtesy of HHRC

Astrodome

I debated whether to include the Eighth Wonder of the World, since it's technically not lost. Yet. The Astrodome was completed in April 1965 as the world's first fully air-conditioned, enclosed indoor domed sports stadium. The centerpiece of Roy "Judge" Hofheinz's Astrodomain, it was established as the home of the Houston Astros baseball team. Over the years it's hosted everything from the Houston Oilers football team to bullfighting and celebrity tennis matches. The dome closed in 2009 and now stands vacant, which isn't doing the old dear any favors. Now and again someone pitches an ambitious idea to save it—such as Gensler's $1 billion redevelopment plan, Vision: Astrodome, unveiled in 2024.

Photos courtesy of HHRC

Courtesy of HHRC

Colt Stadium

When Judge Roy Hofheinz and his crew eventually landed the deal to bring Major League Baseball to Houston in 1960, threatening to create their own league, it all hung on his promise to build the Astrodome. The problem? It takes time to work modern architectural miracles. As a stop-gap, a public naming contest was held, and the nascent Houston baseball team was called the Colt .45s. Colt Stadium, a temporary structure, was built next to the Astrodome construction site. The team played in Colt Stadium from 1962 to 1965, when they moved into the dome and were rebranded the Houston Astros. Colt Stadium was then taken apart and shipped to Mexico.

GOLF COURSES

Fore! Look out for the stories of now-gone Houston golf courses. We could erase strokes from our scorecard, but we can't erase the sunny memories of these classic Houston courses. The now-abandoned Bear Creek Golf World was founded by former Houston Country Club pro Dick Forester. A full gold membership at Inwood Forest Golf and Country Club cost $250 when it opened. The Par 5 ninth hole at the public Glenbrook Golf Course frustrated many a player. And Raveneaux's disappearing act was a local golf tragedy. All these courses gave Houstonians face time with friends, fun challenges, and reasons to get out into the fresh air and sunshine. Long may they live in our memories.

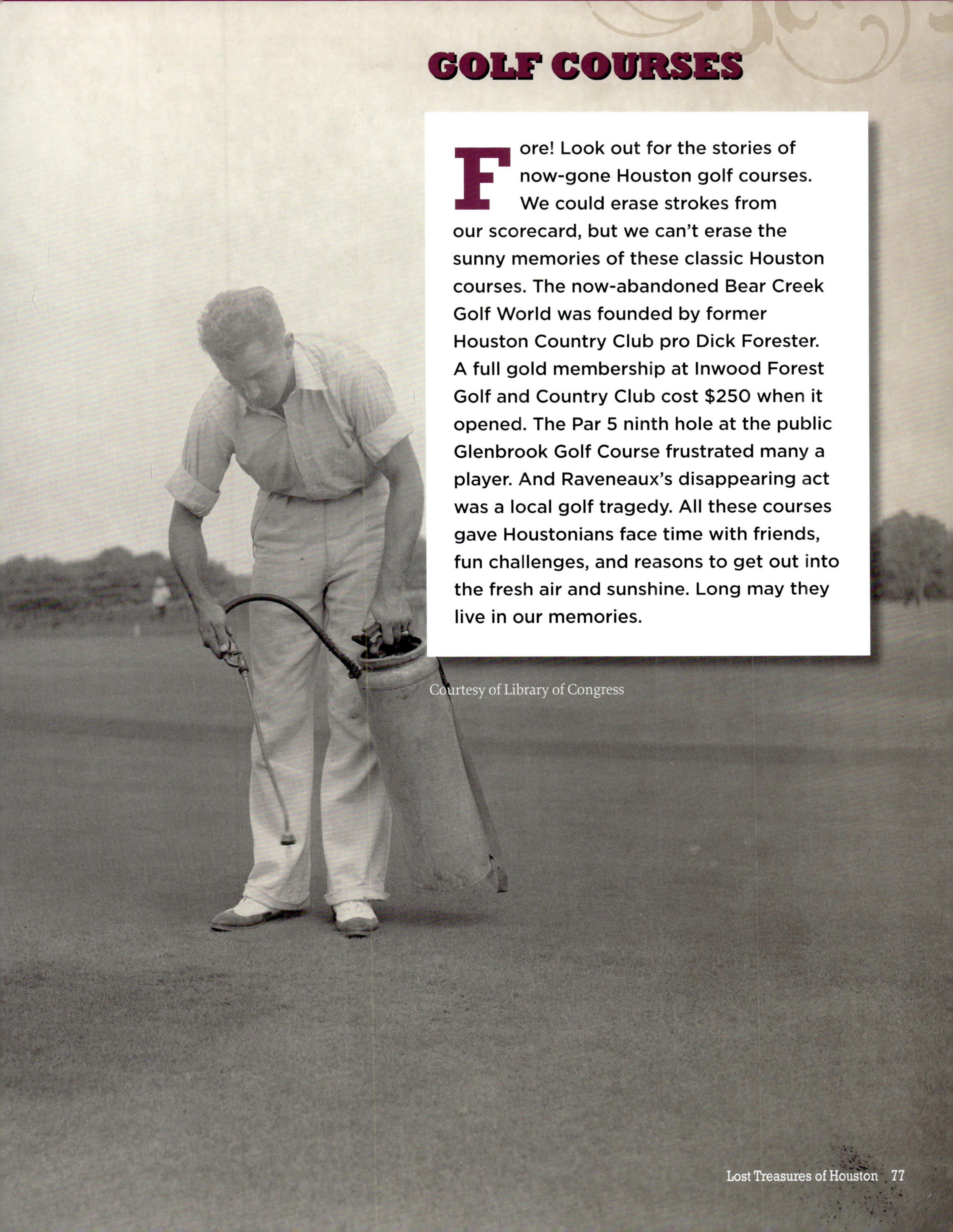

Courtesy of Library of Congress

Bear Creek Golf World

My father and I played a Sunday morning game at Bear Creek for much of my adult life. On Highway 6 at Clay Road, the facility offered three 18-hole courses: Masters, Presidents, and Challenger. The course opened in 1968, designed by Houston-born Jay Riviere, who played on the Rice University golf team and worked to restore the golf course at Memorial Park. It wasn't a neighborhood course, so you didn't have to worry about putting a Titleist through someone's skylight. After Hurricane Harvey destroyed it in 2017, it was not rebuilt. One of the clubhouse bricks sits on my desk.

Inwood Forest Country Club

Also designed by Jay Riviere, Inwood Forest Country Club was at 7603 Antoine Drive. Collier Airport sold a chunk of this semi-rural land to a group of local investors who golfed, and Inwood Forest Country Club teed off in 1967. Pilots would get confused and land on the fairway rather than the runway at first, and in the early days the clubhouse was just a trailer. Players thought it a relatively tough course for its day, though. Eventually it added wonderful tennis and swimming facilities, serving as a social hub for the neighborhood. The club and course closed in 2007; today it's a stormwater detention site.

Courtesy of WhispertoMe

Glenbrook Golf Course

Glenbrook opened in 1935 at 8205 North Bayou Drive right off Sims Bayou East of Interstate 45. Glenbrook started as the Rio Rita Country Club, which featured a nine-hole sand green course. The City of Houston later acquired the property and built an 18-hole course on the site, presumably because sand greens are an affront to God and should not be allowed east of Interstate 35. Glenbrook was a challenging, popular, and affordable municipal course for more than 80 years. In 2018 the city closed Glenbrook to create the beautiful Houston Botanic Gardens on the grounds, to the delight of practically everyone in Houston who doesn't golf.

Courtesy of Jose Luis Rayo

Raveneaux Country Club

At 9415 Cypresswood Drive up in Spring, Raveneaux Country Club was a huge draw in Champions Forest. Designed by Bruce Devlin and Robert von Hagge, who designed courses around the world, Raveneaux opened in 1979. It featured not just a rustic 18-hole golf course but tennis, swimming, and an enormous clubhouse resembling a French chateau. It soon became the area's residential center of gravity. But in 2020, Harris County bought the clubhouse property then, against the wishes of the residents, closed the entire facility in 2021. The clubhouse was demolished, and the property was transformed into a stormwater detention basin.

Courtesy of Benjamin Herarra

{RETAIL}

In a world where it may seem like everyone buys "everything" online, 80 percent of retail purchases are still made at brick-and-mortar shops. So it hurts when Houston-only retail experiences fade away.

During the golden age of department stores—say the late 1880s to the 1960s—independent Houston retailers offered a bespoke, local experience. A lady looking for a new summer hat, students looking for sharp back-to-school shirts and dresses, and businessmen looking to up their image to close the deal were treated like royalty at stores like Foley's, Sakowitz, Battelstein's, Kaplan's Ben Hur, and others. Taking pride in their beautiful buildings and carefully engineered luxurious atmosphere, the department stores of old offered personalized service, elegant cafés, and extravagant holiday experiences.

Houston's past hotels and motels, too, haven't just made guests comfortable—they've made statements. At Glenn McCarthy's lavish Shamrock Hotel, two different water wells were drilled to supply the pool's 177,000 gallons—famously used for indoor water-skiing exhibitions. More practical hotels like the William Penn and Lamar may not have held a grand opening featuring Errol Flynn or Lana Turner, but they did bring comfort and civilization to travelers in an age when travel wasn't always so easy or comfortable.

The way Houstonians bought everyday groceries evolved over time, from the days of Henke & Pillot to the Disco Kroger on Montrose Boulevard.

And, of course, we saw the rise and decline of the big '80s shopping mall, along with its big '80s hair. Generations of Houstonians shopped, ate, flirted, sipped Orange Julius drinks, and for some reason, bought gloves without fingers in them from Chess King, at now-defunct malls all around town.

Then there were the bookstores and other niche retailers. I always just assumed the Half Price Books in the Rice Village would remain a feature of the region's geology over time—even after the ocean retook the Texas coastline. And wonderful, quirky Houston-only places like the Wilde Collection or Kegg's Candies seemed as though they would keep bringing joy and wonder to visitors forever. But, alas, nothing lasts forever—especially in retail. Look upon my works of Kegg's Candies Pecan Clusters, ye mighty, and despair.

Chief Motel
Courtesy of Library of Congress

River Oaks Bookstore Sign
Courtesy of Whitney Andrews Corson

Northwest Mall
Courtesy of Cheryl Czerewaty

Shamrock Pool
Courtesy of HHRC

DEPARTMENT STORES

There's nothing like the elegant atmosphere and bespoke service of an old-school department store. And many class acts have served Houston. Those no longer asking if they can help include Foley's, a part of the Houston community in some way or another for 100+ years. Sakowitz, Kaplan's Ben-Hur, and Battelstein's all treated Houstonians like royalty. Relative newcomers Weiner's and Palais Royal were the home of many a back-to-school shopping trip. Let's browse some of Houston's long-gone department store brands. Third floor, ladies' dresses and blouses! Don't forget our holiday specials.

Courtesy of HHRC

Kaplan's Ben-Hur

Kaplan's at 2129 Yale Street was as much about community as commerce. The Kaplan family originally ran Kaplan's Feed Store and Dry Goods at 2200 Yale in 1913. It was a bit like a Tractor Supply Company, serving a community of semi-rural households. After the area urbanized, the store wound up a trusted mid-century department store in the 1950s. The name was a play on two of the family's brothers, Bennett and Herman. A combination of corporate franchises, discount chains, and online retailing put Kaplan's Ben-Hur out of business in 2005. But its quality goods and exceptional service live on in the hearts of many to this day.

Foley's Downtown

W. L. Foley, who owned a dry goods store on Travis Street in the late 1800s, convinced his nephews to come from Ireland to learn the retail trade. Ireland was still under British rule at the time, so it was probably worth moving for the food alone. By 1900 they had their own store at 1900 Main. They sold the business in 1917, but by then Foley's was perfectly positioned for the golden days of the department store. When its 1100 Main Street location opened in 1947, it epitomized middle-class prosperity—the first Southern store with an escalator. From Christmas display windows to tailored suits, generations of Houstonians grew up with Foley's. Macy's bought the chain in 2006.

Courtesy of HHRC

Sakowitz

Ukrainian-born Tobias and Simon Sakowitz paid their parents for room and board as children. Their parents, however, saved the money and gave it back to them as business capital when they were older. How disciplined and industrious was that? Enter Sakowitz in 1902. By the 1950s, this regional luxury department store helped define high fashion and the good life in Houston and beyond. Ladies could find the latest European fashions, and gentlemen could purchase a fresh new chapeau. Its 1111 Main Street location was designed by famed architect Alfred C. Finn and topped 250,000 luxurious square feet. Tobias's son eventually took over operations, but over time the family fell out, and the chain closed in 1990. Local entrepreneur Jerry Gronauer, who once ran the store's fur department, bought the name and reopened it as "Sakowitz Furs."

Battelstein's

Philip Battelstein had 50 cents upon arrival in the USA from Lithuania in 1870. In 1897, he moved to Houston, where he started a series of modest tailor's shops that eventually grew into one of Houston's premier luxury department store chains. Battelstein's iconic building at 1813 Main Street was built in 1950, and soon the store expanded to other locations, including a store at 2010 South Shepherd Drive that was a cherished part of the River Oaks neighborhood for decades. Battelstein's closed in 1981 after a 1980 sale to Bealls.

Courtesy of HHRC

Weiner's

Isidore Weiner started this popular chain of department stores with a location on Houston Avenue in 1926. The business was a family affair, with several generations pitching in over its life. Located near middle-class neighborhoods, Weiner's wasn't special occasion shopping; it was a part of everyday life. By 1961, Weiner's had racked up 21 stores. At the peak of its popularity, the chain had 50 locations in Houston alone and more than 150 total in Texas and Louisiana. The business started facing financial difficulty in the mid-1990s, and after Tropical Storm Allison hit in 2001 the business flipped around the Closed sign for good.

Courtesy of Weiner's

Palais Royal

This practical chain of department stores was started in 1921 by Milton Levy. His first location was at 620 Main Street—just a single room. In coming decades the business grew, upgraded spaces, and went through a number of owners after Levy's death. Palais Royal sold a variety of reasonably priced clothing for men, women, and kids—as well as shoes, housewares, cosmetics, and more. Eventually the chain would have 80+ locations outside of its flagship downtown store, scattered around Houston neighborhood strip malls and suburbs. Palais Royal was eventually bought by Stage Stores and would close in 2020.

Courtesy of Travis L McIntire

Joske's

This San Antonio–based department store chain was started by German immigrant Julius Joske in 1867—choosing San Antonio because of its military base that constantly needed supplies. It is widely recognized as being the first Texas department store to have air conditioning throughout the whole store (fancy). Joske's came to Houston in 1948 with a location at 407 Main Street—the former site of a Foley's store. This Joske's location mostly sold home goods and had a posh-ish "Garden Room" that offered an agreeable buffet every Monday night. More locations followed, including popular Joske's stores at Gulfgate, Post Oak, Northline, the Galleria, and many of the malls around Houston. The chain sold to Dillard's in 1987. The old building at 407 Main has been demolished.

Best Products

Best Products was a catalog showroom—a retail concept that featured unboxed merchandise buyers could check out before having goods pulled from a warehouse to take home. The business was started in 1957 by Sydney and Francis Lewis of Richmond, Virginia. The couple loved art, and the retail chain generated buzz because of its aesthetic and willingness to actually trade merchandise for art. In the early 1970s, the Lewises commissioned a firm called Sculpture in the Environment to design nine Best Products locations into real-world works of retail art. The second of these buildings was the Houston store at 10765 Kingspoint Road. Preliminary drawings for the store were actually revealed at the MoMA in 1975. A piece named "Intermediate Facade," the distinctive apocalyptic building was dramatically unveiled via helicopter. But by the late 1990s, the store chain had gone bust. Fearing the city would declare Intermediate Facade a landmark, limiting their financial options, the building owners had the famous facade removed.

Courtesy of HHRC

Hotels and Motels

Crisp linens. That precisely made bed. Unlimited hot water. Early hotels were simple but hugely convenient. The William Penn Hotel was more upscale with air conditioning and an actual coffee shop. The extravagant Shamrock Hotel gave Beaumont-born Glenn McCarthy an excuse to throw Houston's biggest party—a grand opening celebration that cost a cool million dollars in 1949. And during the golden age of the motor inn, the mid-century Tidelands served as not just a snazzy place to snooze near Rice and the Med Center but also a pretty hot nightspot. Let's check out the places Houston visitors used to check in.

Courtesy of Erwan Hesry

The Capitol Hotel

From 1837 to 1839, a modest wooden building at Main Street and Texas Avenue served as our nation's capitol building. The Republic of Texas being the nation in question, of course. After Austin was designated the new seat of the Republic following a contentious changeover, the building served mostly as the Capitol Hotel. In 1881 the original building was demolished. A new Capitol Hotel was built on the site, which was renamed the Rice Hotel after William Marsh Rice, who'd bought the hotel but was murdered by his valet not long after. Alfred C. Finn designed the new Rice Hotel, today the Rice apartments, which stands on the old site.

Courtesy of George Dickey Architect

Ben Milam Hotel

The Ben Milam Hotel, designed by Houston architect James Ruskin Bailey, opened in 1926. Traveling salesmen, oil execs, monied migrants, traveling performers, and academics all blew through the Ben Milam's lobby at 1717 Texas Avenue. It was popular not just because it was across from Union Station but also because they'd spent a pretty penny on it for a business hotel. The Ben Milam had comfortable rooms, a coffee shop, a rooftop pool, and, critical in Houston, an advanced cooling and dehumidifying system. Its days were numbered after Union Station closed, though, and the hotel was demolished in 2012.

William Penn Hotel

Built in 1925 at 1423 Texas Avenue, the William Penn Hotel was designed by architect Joseph Finger—who also designed beautiful art deco structures such as City Hall and Houston's first airport terminal. The 10-story hotel offered an upscale experience catering to traveling businessmen. It featured amenities that were exceptional in its day, such as 24-hour air conditioning, a coffee shop, and even a parking garage. Built by Tellepsen Construction Company, its 152 rooms featured terrazzo and tile. Many had private baths, also a big deal in the day. The William Penn waned as the decades passed, fell vacant by the 1990s, and was demolished in 2006.

Courtesy of Boston Public Library

Lamar Hotel

Built by Jesse Jones in 1927, the Lamar Hotel at 1200 Main Street wasn't just luxurious; it was influential. Especially noteworthy was "Suite 8F," a meeting place for powerful Texas businessmen and politicians. Rented by Herman and George R. Brown, of Brown & Root fame, the room was used to broker deals with impact not just on Houston but the world. On any given afternoon you might find the governor or the leader of a major oil company in negotiations over cards and whiskey. The Lamar was demolished in 1985, but in many ways, the legacy of the 8F crowd lives on.

Shamrock Hotel

Wildcatter Glenn McCarthy's eccentric Shamrock Hotel opened on St. Patrick's Day of 1949 with a lavish launch party that included the Texas governor, Hollywood movie stars, reporters from around the country, and a 22-piece orchestra. On the corner of Main Street and West Holcombe Boulevard, the massive luxury hotel had a 1,100 guest capacity, several bars and restaurants, and a swimming pool big enough to water ski in (which they did). The interior featured 63 unique shades of green, and a national radio show called "Saturday at the Shamrock" was broadcast from the hotel. It sold to Hilton in 1955, but its size and distance from downtown at the time were its downfall. The Shamrock was demolished in 1987.

Courtesy of Boston Public Library

Tidelands Motor Inn

Built in 1958, the Tidelands Motor Inn at 6500 South Main was a 200-room motor court across the street from Rice University. The manager, Dick Meagle, played football at Rice, and professionally for the San Francisco 49ers. Billing itself as "the ultimate in luxury resort atmosphere," the Tidelands was an upscale take on the motor court, complete with nightlife. It had a nightclub at which acts such as Bob Newhart, Jonathan Winters, and the Smothers Brothers performed. A second location was built at 6700 Main. But eventually the glamour faded, and the Tidelands was purchased by Rice University for student housing.

The Savoy Hotel

The Savoy Hotel at 1616 Main Street was built in 1906 to take advantage of the oil boom. In 1909 it became Houston's first high-rise apartment, though only seven stories. The Savoy served as home to many Houstonians over the decades. Historians say Lee Harvey Oswald stayed there while in town to interview for a job with Conoco; I'll bet that made for an interesting interview. A 17-story addition was built in 1966. By the late 1980s the Savoy stood vacant. In 2009, the original structure was demolished, while the annex became a Holiday Inn.

Chief Motel

Courtesy of John Margolies

Post-WWII prosperity paired with a shiny new federal highway system and car culture writ large brought about a golden age of roadside motels. A sense of adventure took hold, and places like the Chief Motel at 9000 South Main (at Broadmead) were there for it. With its high-profile neon sign meant to snag motorists with heavy eyelids and its distinctively mid-century design sensibility, it was a prime example of its breed—offering clean, affordable rooms to working-class travelers on the go. The Chief lasted several decades, drawing in customers with its location right across from the Astrodome. But as the years wore on, chain hotels began snapping up the market share. Interstates made older routes, and their motels, obsolete. And cheap, miserable flights by discount airlines chipped away at Peak Road Trip. The Chief Motel was torn town in 2017. Today there's a Staybridge Suites at the location.

MARKETS

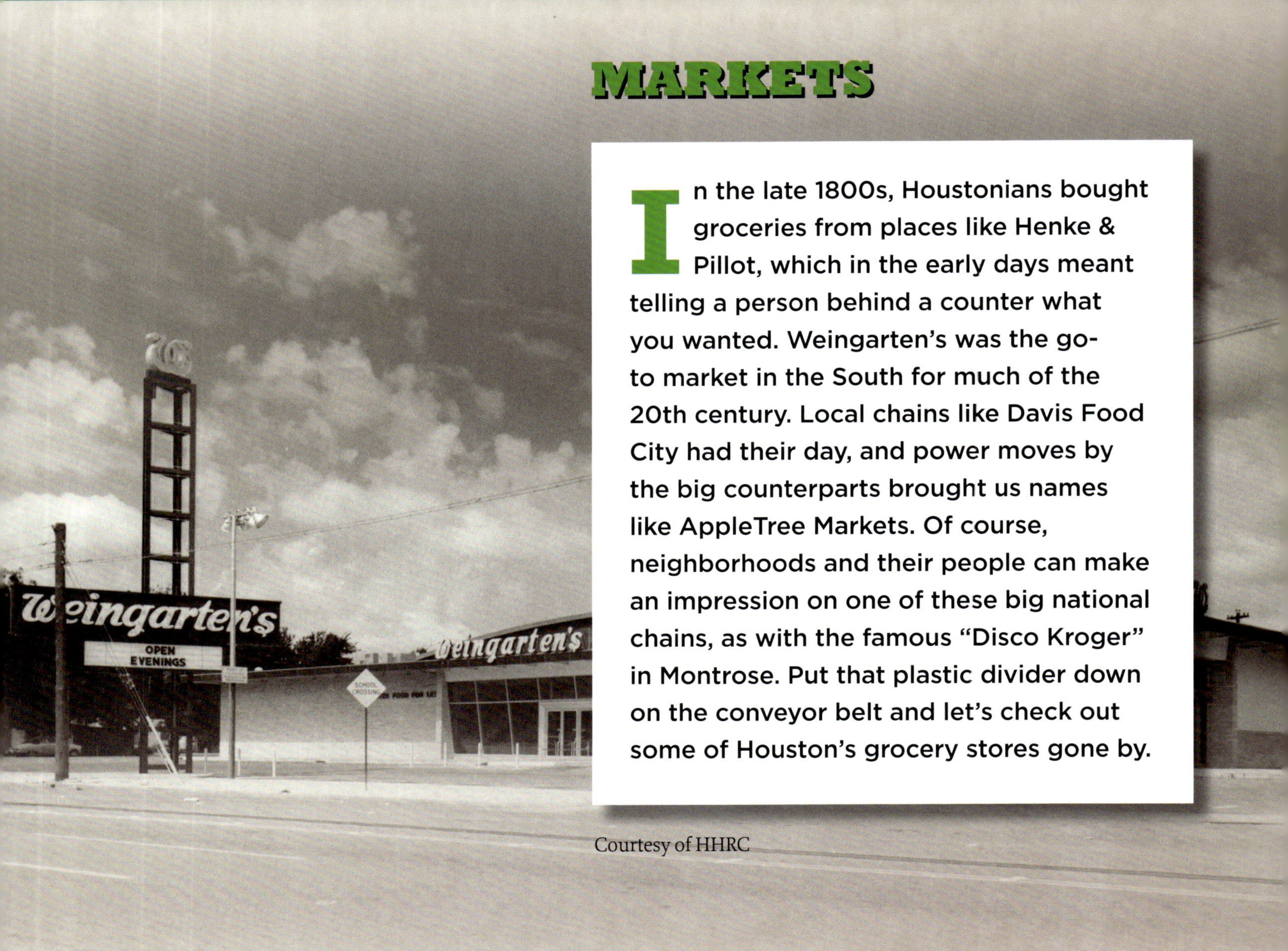

In the late 1800s, Houstonians bought groceries from places like Henke & Pillot, which in the early days meant telling a person behind a counter what you wanted. Weingarten's was the go-to market in the South for much of the 20th century. Local chains like Davis Food City had their day, and power moves by the big counterparts brought us names like AppleTree Markets. Of course, neighborhoods and their people can make an impression on one of these big national chains, as with the famous "Disco Kroger" in Montrose. Put that plastic divider down on the conveyor belt and let's check out some of Houston's grocery stores gone by.

Courtesy of HHRC

Weingarten's

At one time, if you said you were going to get groceries anywhere around Southeast Texas, that meant you were probably going to Weingarten's. Father and son Harris and Joseph Weingarten opened the first H. Weingarten's store at Congress Avenue and Crawford Street. By the time of Joseph Weingarten's death in 1967 the business had 70 locations in Texas and other states. The chain was bought by Grand Union in the 1970s. But the merger wasn't a happy marriage, and Weingarten's grocery stores would go out of business in the 1980s; its real estate arm would be acquired in 2021.

HENKE & PILLOT

German-born Henry Henke learned the retail trade from his brother at a store in New Orleans as the War Between the States was winding down. After moving to Galveston, then Houston, and doing well in a number of ventures, he opened Henke & Pillot in 1892—taking on the company's bookkeeper as a partner. By 1951 the store had 20+ locations. Kroger merged with Henke & Pillot in the mid-1950s, making it a Kroger subsidiary. Kroger let the business run under its own brand for a time, but eventually the Henke & Pillot brand would become just an all-but-forgotten aspect of a long-gone merger. *Leb wohl für immer*, Henke & Pillot.

Courtesy of Henke & Pillot

Courtesy of Bruce Godwin

Courtesy of Robert Snoza

The "Disco Kroger"

The Kroger at 3300 Montrose Boulevard wasn't *officially* called that, this *nom commercial* having been coined by Houston author Jeff Balke. Still, built in 1978, the store did play disco back in the day. Also in modern days, come to think of it, until its 2021 closing. A late-night store in a vibrant LGBTQ+ neighborhood, it was filled with eccentric party people doing eccentric party things. If, after leaving Numbers at 2 a.m., you needed groceries to make salmon eggs benedict for six while listening to "Tainted Love" by Soft Cell, this was your store. Not to be confused with Atlanta's Disco Kroger.

Davis Food City

Albert Leo Davis was a South Carolinian who started and scaled his successful grocery store chain while living in Fort Worth. By 1962, the store had 50 locations, eight of which were in the Houston area. But by growing too quickly, Davis had gotten a bit over his skis. His books loaded with unsustainable debt, Davis's wife took desperate measures and sold all of her stock in the company—giving the proceeds to her husband to immediately lose in Las Vegas. His would be a comeback story, though, eventually moving to Houston and growing the discount Food City chain before his passing in 2023. Who doesn't love a good comeback story?

Courtesy of Ilo Frey

AppleTree Markets

Courtesy of Tara Clark

AppleTree was formed to snap up about 50 former Safeway locations after a hostile takeover. The idea was that this new, big beast could take on the bigger Randalls and Kroger chains by targeting the middle class, cutting costs, creating efficiencies, and optimizing its real estate equity. But the competition from these bigger businesses proved insurmountable, and AppleTree just didn't have the economies of scale that Safeway and the others had enjoyed. The last AppleTree market in Houston closed in 1997, but its final surviving store in Bryan made it all the way to 2010 before shutting its doors.

RETAIL CENTERS AND MALLS

Gadzooks. Spencer's Gifts. KB Toys. If you're experiencing this book through reading glasses, you might have grown up during the peak mall years of the late 1970s, 1980s, and early 1990s. Was it commerce masquerading as culture? Honestly, between the El Chico, the video game arcade, and the knife store that sported a whole jewelry case of ninja throwing stars, 13-year-old me didn't care. As we move into the age of online shopping, several Houston malls have gone to the great Merry-Go-Round beyond, including Greenspoint, Northwest, Westwood, and Town & Country. Let's get on our mall-walking shoes and revisit them.

Courtesy of Library of Congress

Westbury Square

Designed by architect William Wortham to resemble an Old World European village, Westbury Square was an instantly popular shopping destination when it opened in 1962. Developer Ira Berne also built the Westbury neighborhood. The shopping center at Chimney Rock and West Bellfort Avenue would elevate the area by pulling together 60 wonderfully eclectic restaurants and shops. Berne was an Italophile and imported the center's piazza fountain from Italy. But no fountain could compete with the Galleria's air conditioning and lack of summer mosquitoes. Westbury Square began a slow spiral in the 1970s and, as of this writing, is an abandoned ruin awaiting the wrecking ball.

Westwood Mall

Opening in 1975, Westwood Mall was at the Southwest Freeway and Bissonnet Street. In the 1970s, this part of town was a high-growth area, and this two-story mall had all of the Big Mall accoutrements in demand at the time, ranging from big anchor stores like Sears and JCPenney to a Gold Mine arcade, a Spencer's Gifts, and an Orange Julius. It looked so much like your typical 1980s mall that a 1983 made-for-TV movie about a boy's kidnapping, *Adam* starring JoBeth Williams, filmed scenes there. A combination of crime and competition would eventually force Westwood Mall's closure and repurposing.

Courtesy of Judah Davis

NORTHWEST MALL

Northwest Mall opened in the fall of 1968 at the intersection of Loop 610 and Highway 290. It was a prosperous mall in its day, with all of the requisite big department stores, a free-standing cinema, a Farrell's Ice Cream, and dozens of other reasons to visit. Today the mall is boarded up and falling down. Proponents of a high-speed Houston-to-DFW rail development want the space as a rail terminus. Reactions to the repurposing have been mixed, however; among the loudest critics have been landowners between Houston and Dallas whose private property has been targeted by sketchy government seizure schemes.

Courtesy of Cheryl Czerewaty

Greenspoint Mall

OK, let's get this out of the way: Yes, everybody called that mall "Gunspoint" because of the crime. But it wasn't always so. Originally Greenspoint Mall was a very nice place to shop. It had Battelstein's, Foley's, Montgomery Ward, Joske's, Sears, and even Lord & Taylor in later years. You could pick up some parachute pants at Chess King or a TRS 1000 computer at Radio Shack, maybe go catch *The Terminator* at the Greenspoint General Cinema Center 5. But in the summer of 2024 the leases of the last of its tenants were themselves terminated. The city is looking to develop part of the property into affordable housing.

Courtesy of Judah Davis

Town & Country Mall

In 1983 the north end of the Town & Country Village shopping complex was developed into the Town & Country Mall. In the 1980s, the west side of Houston was growing quickly, and Town & Country grew with it. With Neiman Marcus and Saks Fifth Avenue as big anchor stores, many west side residents preferred to do their shopping at Town & Country rather than the Galleria so they didn't have to deal with Galleria parking. By the 2000s, though, the place was run down, and tenants were scarce. It was demolished in 2005, and today the prominent CityCentre complex stands in its place.

BOOKSTORES

There's a case to be made that in an era wherein digital puppet masters can manipulate online information at will, bookstores matter more than ever before—bringing people together, propagating ideas, and building community. Sadly, Houston has lost some good ones over the years, from the dusty stacks of the Half Price Books in the Rice Village to the charming, bespoke service and neighborhood feel of River Oaks Bookstore. History may have turned the page on Houston's lost bookstores, but we can still honor them and the joy they brought us. Let's revisit a few of many.

Courtesy of WhispertoMe

River Oaks Bookstore

The lovely Jeanne Jard opened River Oaks Bookstore in the early 1970s, the store growing into a hub for everyone in the area with a passion for reading. They sold quality books and hosted a number of prominent authors. Jard's son, Mike Jones, took over a few decades in, but Jeanne remained a beloved fixture. Everyone there was just so kind; neighbors came in for a chat as much as a book. When I had a signing there that didn't pull much of a crowd, employees plied me with much-appreciated wine. After 47 years in business, the bookstore closed in 2020 due to the coronavirus shutdowns.

Courtesy of Whitney Andrews Corson

Half Price Books Rice Village

Opening its doors at 2537 University Boulevard in the early 1980s, the Half Price Books in the Rice Village was a Houston favorite. The building had once been a department store; you can still see the "Meyer Bros. White House Store" logo on the floor tiles out front. The Village Half Price Books thrived for decades, earning loyal patronage from not just students but diverse groups of frugal Houston book buyers. I remember it had a wonderful winding staircase leading to the upper level. But as the area gentrified, rents increased. It was finally priced out of the Rice Village, and out of business, in March 2020.

Half Price Books in Montrose

The Montrose Half Price Books at 1011 Westheimer Road opened in 2002. For almost 20 years it served as not just a great place to pick up your latest read within walking distance but also a community hub in the area with strong hangout energy. The eclectic, artsy, and historically progressive Montrose was perfect for a used bookstore like this—where it's about the browsing as much as it's about the books themselves. Not only was it a great location, but customers loved the staff. And the store always seemed to have a generous inventory. But development and the overall gentrification of the area doomed the location. A New York–based commercial real estate developer purchased the land housing the strip center in which the bookstore operated. The Montrose Half Price Books shut down shortly after the closing of HPB's Rice Village location.

Courtesy of Mario Pina Fuentes

Barnes & Noble
7626 Westheimer

Of course, the world's largest retail bookseller is still going strong (big thanks for carrying my books). But the old Westheimer location at 7626 Westheimer Road near Voss was a Galleria-area favorite for 20+ years. Part of the Westheimer Crossing shopping center, the 38,700-square-foot store opened in 1996. It was beloved by residents of Briarmeadow, Tanglewilde, Piney Point, and other neighborhoods. And combined with the other stores in Westheimer Crossing, it made for great holiday shopping. Today the old bookstore building is the new location of Collectors Firearms, "the best damn gunshop in the world." As of this writing there is a tank parked out front, which doesn't involve books but many will admit is kind of fun.

Domy Books

While in business for only seven years, Domy Books made a real impact on the Houston art scene. Founded by Russell Etchen, Domy Books at 1709 Westheimer was a bookstore with strong creative opinions—bringing the latest in progressive art and culture to shoppers. It also served as a gallery space. Minimalist and well-curated, the store became a hub for Houston artists serious about culture and their craft. Plus, it was right next to the Brasil Café. Etchen also opened a Domy in Austin, but by 2013 both locations had shut their doors. Today 1709 Westheimer is home to Flatland Gallery.

Courtesy of Robert Boyd

RETAIL STORES

James Gulliver once quipped, "Retail is detail." The old Jive Hive/Record Rack orchestrated a million details to bring not just great music but celebrity—and a sense of family—to customers. Sales associates at I W Marks Jewelers made many a young bride-to-be's dreams come true. And before its tragic closing, one look into the Wilde Collection told you its owners carefully curated every bizarre, wonderful item in the store. Here are a few bygone Houston retailers that always looked after the little things to make a big impression on Houston's history.

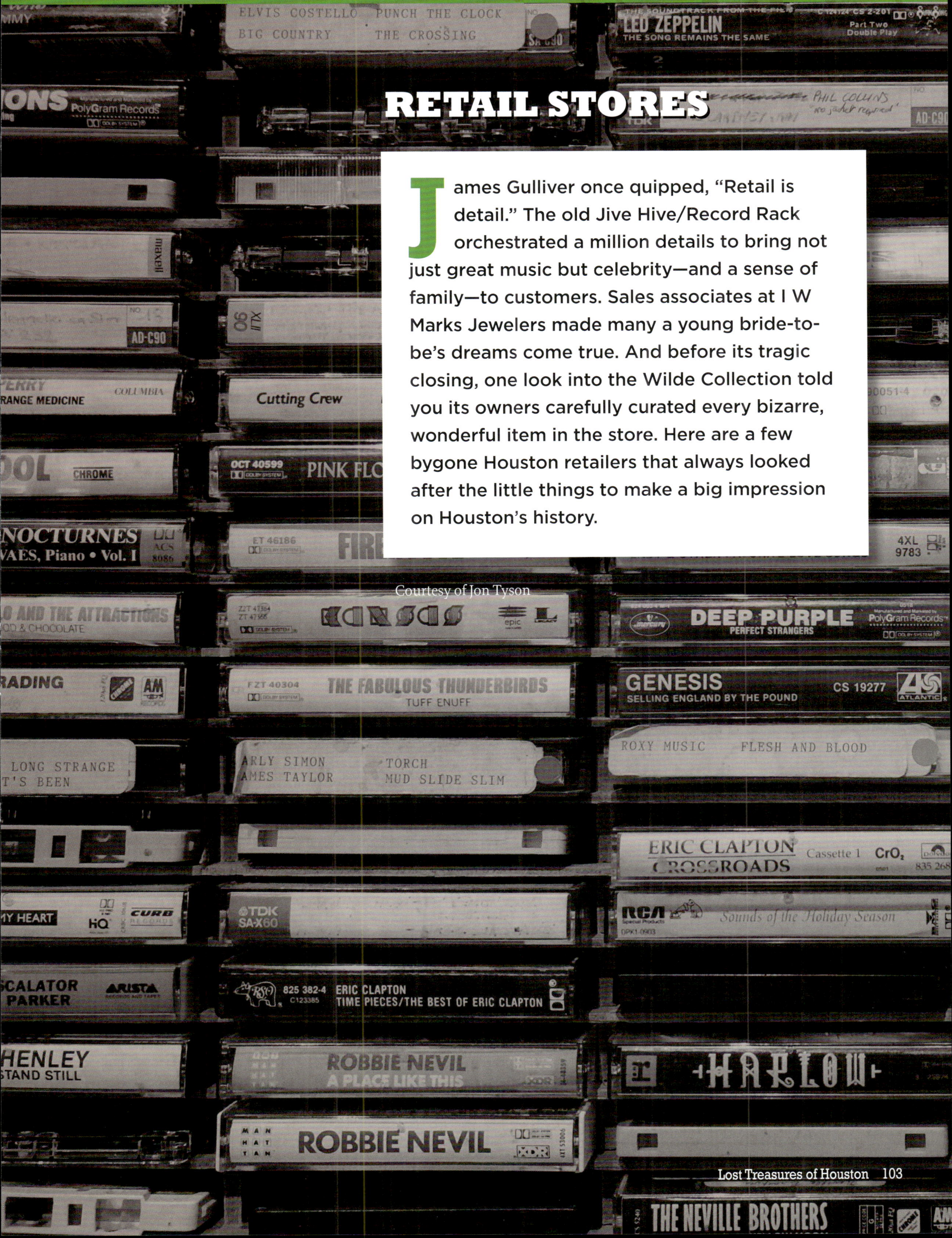

Courtesy of Jon Tyson

Hastings

Hastings sold books, CDs, records, DVDs, posters, T-shirts, collectibles, and all kinds of other fun stuff. They had locations around the edges of Houston but preferred to serve smaller towns, suburbs, and college towns. Founded by Sam Marmaduke of Amarillo in 1968, Hastings Entertainment started as the retail arm of a books and music wholesaler called Western Merchandisers. By the time it went public in 1998, it had more than 120 stores. But you didn't buy this book at Hastings because the Marmaduke family eventually sold the business, which struggled in a post-Amazon world. By 2016 Hastings was a has-been.

Courtesy of Bruce Godwin

The Record Rack

The Record Rack, originally called the Jive Hive, opened in 1957 at 3109 South Shepherd. It was rebranded when John and Helen Flintjer bought it in 1982. Eventually, the store was purchased by Bruce Godwin—who also owned the popular Numbers nightclub for a time, which is still going strong! By the 1980s, the Record Rack wasn't just a music store; it was an adjunct to the local club scene. Godwin stocked the music he liked, and many in the neighborhood shared his taste. Morrissey, the Pet Shop Boys, and Ministry all visited the Record Rack—as did the Village People. The store closed in 2002, but the love so many had for the store and what it represented lives on through the lives of many.

The Original Christmas Store

Before one could walk into the At Home decor superstore in Katy and get lost in floor-to-ceiling Christmas cheer, Houston had the Original Christmas Store. Founded by the Grubich family of Dallas, it came on the local scene in 1974. You could go any time of the year, but people flocked in during the holidays to pick up nativity scenes, Christmas tree decorations, wreaths, gifts, and other holiday decor. Many families made a visit to the Original Christmas Store part of their post-Thanksgiving family traditions, not only to shop but also to see its elaborate holiday displays. The Houston store closed in the late 1990s through a combination of rising rents on Westheimer Road and big box store competition.

I W Marks Jewelers

Diane and Irv Marks founded this upscale jewelry store at 3841 Bellaire Boulevard in 1978. You could buy a Rolex or some diamond earrings many places. But Irv Marks made his customers feel special with bespoke service, custom designs, and a feeling that you were a part of something bigger than the jewelry itself. Irv was often the face of the business, especially its marketing, though sons Brad and Daniel opened a second store in Sugar Land in 2004. Irv Marks passed in 2008 after a battle with cancer, with Brad taking the helm until the business's closing in 2023.

Finger Furniture

Latvian-born Sam Finger bought land and a store in Shepherd, Texas, before retiring in Houston. While here he started a side gig renting out appliances during the Great Depression when the concept of having $100 to buy a refrigerator was preposterous to many hard-working Texans. Eventually he started Finger Furniture, which would stay in the family for 80+ years. Its flagship location was at 4001 Gulf Freeway, the former site of Buffalo Stadium (home plate was memorialized inside the store at a sports museum). It became Ashley Furniture for a time but finally closed for good in 2014. The family's Finger Farm is still going in Shepherd.

Courtesy of Brian Merzbach

Wilde Collection

What a weird, wonderful treasure was the Wilde Collection. A sort of quirky cabinet of dark curiosities, the Wilde Collection at 1446 Yale Street opened in 2015—showcasing and selling oddities that included bizarrely taxidermied animals, Victorian jewelry, medical antiques, and other fascinations. It was inspired by both Oscar Wilde and Edgar Allan Poe. To me it felt like an archetypical mystic shop that could have been found in an episode of Roald Dahl's *Tales of the Unexpected* or Rod Serling's *The Twilight Zone*. Tragically, the store was lost at the hands of an arsonist in 2019.

Courtesy of Lawyer B Douglas II

Kegg's Candies

Founder Robert Kegg opened this local candy shop in 1946, with the store's first location in the Rice Village. Kegg's made high-quality, old-fashioned candy with locally sourced ingredients. And they were serious about quality. The store's glass display cases boasted all manner of chocolate and other treats including pecan crisp, fudge, peanut brittle, caramels, almond bark, a number of things dipped in chocolate ranging from graham crackers to fruit, meltaways made with all kinds of nuts, and "Texas snails," which featured rolled layers of caramel and marshmallow. Kegg's had two locations, one on Westpark and the other on Beechnut, when it closed in July 2018.

Courtesy of HistoricFinds01

{MEDIA}

A city's media landscape is a reflection of its citizenry, and for that reason alone Houston with its constant change has burned through its share of newspapers, radio stations, and television channels. And, of course, nothing and nobody escapes the ravages of time. Except, somehow, my wife. Or Jason Bateman.

Speaking of people who never seemed to age, beloved author and newspaper columnist Leon Hale wrote thousands of pieces between the *Houston Post* and the *Houston Chronicle*. He loved a good road trip and wrote many tales of tramping up and down Lone Star blacktop. Flamboyant Marvin Zindler, who had his own radio program covering Houston crime scenes in the 1940s, was a Houston institution for decades. Ron Stone kept Houstonians credibly informed for many, many years—and even wrote three books on Texas history.

Legendary radio DJ Paul Berlin, who hated Billy Joel's "She's Always a Woman" so much he smashed his radio station's copy, kept Houston dancing. Of course, if you danced in the wrong place, your family might have wound up calling Ray Hill's The Prison Show radio program. Rumor that Mark Stevens's and Jim Pruett's popular talk radio Uncle Waldo character served time in Huntsville couldn't be substantiated by the Lost Treasures research team. But if you held a fancy enough fundraiser to get him out, you might have spotted the tuxedoed Alvin Van Black in the crowd giving the rest of us a look in.

Houstonians read the Post, then the Post and the Chronicle, then just the Chronicle. Then, eventually, maybe the Chrome app on your phone. Radio stations came and went, with the Rock station KKRW playing its last classic rock jam in 2013 and eventually becoming 93.7 The Beat.

In recent years different factors have reshaped the media landscape, not just in Houston but around the world. Trust in media institutions isn't great right now, with Gallup reporting just 31 percent of Americans expressing "a great deal" or "fair amount" of confidence in the media. And technology, especially for younger Houstonians, who get their news from places like TikTok and Instagram, are redefining media preferences as you read this. Fun fact: Grizzy's Hood News has a million followers on Facebook (respect).

Ray Hill
Courtesy of us006409

Leon Hale
Courtesy of Babette Hale

Ron Stone and Leopold Meyer
Courtesy of HHRC

THE HOUSTON POST: WEDNESDAY MORNING, JUNE 1, 1921.

HOUSTON POST SPORTS

Houston Post Swimming Campaign Starts June 6

Another American Woman Golfer Is Eliminated

Trophy For Big Race Numbered Same As Winner's Car

FOUND

ENTRY BLANK

RICE BANQUET TO BE STAGED FRIDAY FOR ALL LETTER MEN

ARBITRATOR NAMED TO DECIDE WINNER OF WRESTLING BOUT

Texans Win From Sixth Ward in Last Inning Rally

Harris County League Managers Meet Thursday

Gulf Coast Club Appoints Sports Editor to Solve Much Disputed Point

Special Meeting of the Pasadena Baseball Team

SPORT PICKUPS

Guest Outpoints Leon At Houston A. A. Show

SLIDEWELL SOFT COLLARS

MADE FOR THE B.V.D. BEST RETAIL TRADE

This Is The B. V. D. Label

Foley & Courtney

Men! Choice Suit $14.85

HOUSTONIANS $9

A Live Fashion for Young Men at a Good "Old-Time" Buckley Price! Nine Dollars

Buckley Shoe Co.

French Woman Wins Her Match in Tennis Tourney

BASEBALL TODAY HOUSTON vs. WICHITA FALLS

KQBT Logo
Courtesy of Nakita Kelley

1921 *Houston Post*
Courtesy of Abilene Library Consortium

CELEBRITIES

Houston's bygone media celebrities weren't just part of an industry; they were part of our lives. Many Houstonians grew up reading an actual newspaper with their coffee in the morning, the *Post* or the *Chronicle*. And many of those took a break from global news to read Leon Hale's homespun takes. Television news icons like Marvin Zindler and Alvin Van Black kept us plugged into the world around us. And in the heyday of shock jock radio, Stevens and Pruett made us laugh out loud during our otherwise crumby commutes. So let's celebrate just a few of Houston's many treasured media stars.

Courtesy of HHRC

Ray Hill
(1940–2018)

A self-styled "citizen provocateur," native Houstonian Ray Hill was an activist for LGBTQ+ rights and just underdogs and free speech in general. Before it was trendy, Hill fought on the front lines of the gay rights movement. After having spent four years in prison in the 1970s, he also became an advocate for the incarcerated. His 90.1 KPFT radio program *The Prison Show* let the families of those locked up get information and words of encouragement to their loved ones behind bars. While he lived his final years in penury, his activism inspired many Houstonians.

Ron Stone (1936–2008)

Courtesy of Ron Stone Jr.

Many people today seem to get their news from a combination of Reddit, stand-up comics, and TikTok. But during Ron Stone's day, broadcast TV news anchors were seen as important figures in helping your household figure out what was going on in the world. For four decades, Oklahoma-born Stone kept Houstonians abreast of goings on through both KHOU and KPRC. He spoke with credibility but never pretentiousness, signing off with, "Good night, neighbors." A history buff, he also covered the fall of the Berlin Wall, hosted *The Eyes of Texas*, and wrote several books. Good night, Mr. Stone.

Marvin Zindler (1921–2007)

Many know Zindler from his famous 1973 investigation of the Chicken Ranch brothel in La Grange. But in Houston we also know him as the eccentric consumer advocate for ABC affiliate KTRK-TV. His weekly restaurant coverage made less-than-diligent restaurateurs awake in a cold sweat for decades, lest their rats or slime in the ice machine be made public. Of course, he was more than his public persona; he was also a US Marine, a law enforcement officer, a 33rd-degree Mason, and a member of Congregation Beth Israel. If he wasn't a Houston treasure, there never was one.

Courtesy of University of Houston Libraries

Leon Hale
(1921-2021)

Known for his homespun prose and keen insights, Hale was a prominent Houston storyteller, newspaper columnist, and author. Born in Stephenville, the Texas Tech graduate settled in Houston, where he made a name for himself at the *Houston Post* from 1947 to 1985. This alone would have been an amazing career, but Hale went on to join the *Houston Chronicle*, where he would continue to be a prominent man of letters until 2014. He was the author of 13 books over the years. Elite essayist Phillip Lopate called Hale "among the top three columnists writing in America today." The city is just a little less "Texas" without him.

Courtesy of Babette Hale

Paul Berlin
(1930–2017)

A legend across the Houston radio waves, Memphis-born Paul Berlin's career as a DJ influenced many Houstonians at a time when broadcast radio was at the height of its power; radio audiences felt like they knew the people playing their music. Berlin came to Houston in 1950 and joined KNUZ (also a lost treasure). There, Berlin would play everything from Bob Wills to Bobby Vinton during his time at the station until 1974. Throughout his career, he would go on to DJ at KQUE, KSEV, and KBME, and even continued working after his retirement in 2004.

Mark Stevens (1934–2010) and Jim Pruett (1944–2016)

Courtesy of Kristi Jay

Mark Stevens and Jim Pruett helped pioneer morning format shock jock radio—not just in Southeast Texas but across the nation. Best known for *The Stevens & Pruett Show* on Rock 101 KLOL in the '80s and '90s, their program combined irreverent humor and commentary with pranks, sexual innuendo, skits, and popular rock music. Commuters around town passed the time listening to the duo and their cast of supporting talent deliver bawdy humor, Uncle Waldo sketches, and the latest rock music. The team also gave back through their nonprofit ranch. Check out the documentary *Runaway Radio* for more on that scene from back in the day. *studio applause*

Alvin Van Black (1939–2001)

Native Houstonian Alvin Van Black was a popular radio talk show host and television presenter who drove a number of popular programs over the years. What I remember most was his "Alvin at Night" television segments on ABC affiliate KTRK Channel 13. The show featured Van Black popping up all over town at lavish fundraisers, award shows, theaters, art galleries, private parties, and who-knows-where-else. He wore a trademark tuxedo and was the everyman's gateway to what the great and good around town were doing after hours. If he showed up at your party, you'd done something right.

NEWSPAPERS

Again, many of these categories could have been a book on their own. Newspapers have come and gone in this town like paper license plates: The original *Houston Press*. The *Houston Post*, of course, the big lost paper that stands out in the minds of many Houstonians. There was the *Houston Daily Times,* the *Houston Telegraph*, the *Houston Daily Mercury*, the *Houston Daily Journal*, the *Houston Informer*, and countless others, including many foreign-language newspapers such as the German Texas *Deutsche Zeitung*. But the most prominent of the newspapers of H-town's past were probably the old *Houston Post* and *Houston Press*. So let's unfold these classic broadsheets and "read all about it."

Courtesy of HHRC

Houston Post

For many generations of Houstonians, this was a two-newspaper town: you got either the *Chronicle* (evening) or the *Post* (morning). Founded in 1880, the *Houston Post* was the city's #1 selling newspaper for 115 years. It was started by Gail Borden Johnson. Yes, those Bordens; he's credited with inventing condensed milk. Over the years the *Houston Post* went through several owners and iterations; at its peak more than 300,000 Houstonians made the *Post* part of their daily routine. In 1995, the *Houston Post* was sold to the Hearst Corporation, which also owns the *Chronicle*. It shut down that same year and is now nothing but a media memory.

Courtesy of Library of Congress

THE ORIGINAL *Houston Press*

While Houston did have two big newspapers for many years, there was actually a more salacious third: The *Houston Press*. Not to be confused with today's online *Houston Press*, where you can find concert reviews and such, the old *Houston Press* was a Scripps Howard newspaper. Originally known for calling out local politicians, it was gritty and pretty spicy for an American newspaper of its day. Still, it paid for a murderers' row of talent. Walter Cronkite worked there for a time. Marvin Zindler worked there as a photographer on the crime beat. But it's a tough business, and the old *Press* was acquired by the *Chronicle* in 1964.

Courtesy of Wikimedia Commons

RADIO

Houston's first radio station, WKEV, was broadcast in 1922 from an auto garage at McKinney and San Jacinto Streets. It folded in just two years, making way for KPRC. I love learning new things, and one of the many things I learned writing this book was that a lot of the radio stations I thought had vanished merely shifted times, channels, or formats. Some are online-only (like the old 91.7 KUHA classical station, or the internet revamp of Rock 101 KLOL) or daytime only (like KIKK "Sounds like Texas"). But one station lost for good was 93.7 KKRW, "The Arrow."

Courtesy of Firkin Cat

Courtesy of eposterboy

KKRW The Arrow

The call letters for Houston's FM 93.7 were changed to KKRW at the end of 1993—the fifth designation of the station's life since originally airing in 1964. Branded "The Arrow," for more than a decade this was where Houston turned for classic rock for those who are now getting things in the mail from AARP—Led Zeppelin, Pink Floyd, Fleetwood Mac, AC/DC, and other such musical fare. The Arrow also offered a number of popular radio personalities and programs like Dean & Rog and Walton & Johnson. In 2014, the Arrow became KQBT, 93.7 The Beat. Its last song as a rock format station was "Don't Stop Believin'" by Journey.

{COMMUNITY}

Sure, we're all regularly chased into our homes by mosquitos. We've all seen that elected power is nice, but Jim "Mattress Mack" McIngvale is on a whole other level. And we all stock up on hurricane supplies like we're on an episode of *Doomsday Preppers*. But it takes more than today's shared experiences to make Houston a community. It takes sharing the experiences of yesteryear as well. And everyone reading this might have done things that are pure "Houston" to which many of us can relate.

Many Houstonians have earned a chestful of merit badges at Camp Strake, had their birthday announced by Kitirik on ABC 13, or seen the Von Erichs wrestle at the Sam Houston Coliseum.

You might have shared many quirky icons with friends and family, from pointing out the old Gulf Lollipop sign downtown (for Houstonians of a certain age) to randomly "burping the bayou" with Dean Ruck's now-gone art project. You might have cheered on race cars downtown, or rambled by moonlight via bicycle dressed in an outrageous Halloween costume. Or you might have put "Luv Ya Blue" stickers on your vehicle and cried out in agony at the 1993 AFC Wild Card loss known as "The Choke."

Many have cheered on local celebs who've made it big, whether in Road House or the White House. You might have taken a class on how to do your taxes from Leisure Learning. Many Houstonians took high-flying jobs at Enron or Stanford Financial, regularly flew Continental, or saw concerts at the Summit.

All of these shared experiences from the past have helped connect us today, share the city's culture with newcomers, and lay the groundwork for all the wild, weird, and wonderful things to come here in Houston. Let's take a look back at yesterday's Houston and all the treasures that have fallen by the wayside over the years.

SRV Car at the Art Car Museum

Steve McNair Baseball Card and Houston Oilers Memorabilia

George and Barbara Bush
Courtesy of Laura Patterson

Sam Houston Zephyr Advertisement
Courtesy of Burlington and Rock Island Railroads

Houston Rockets Game Ticket
Courtesy of Houston Rockets

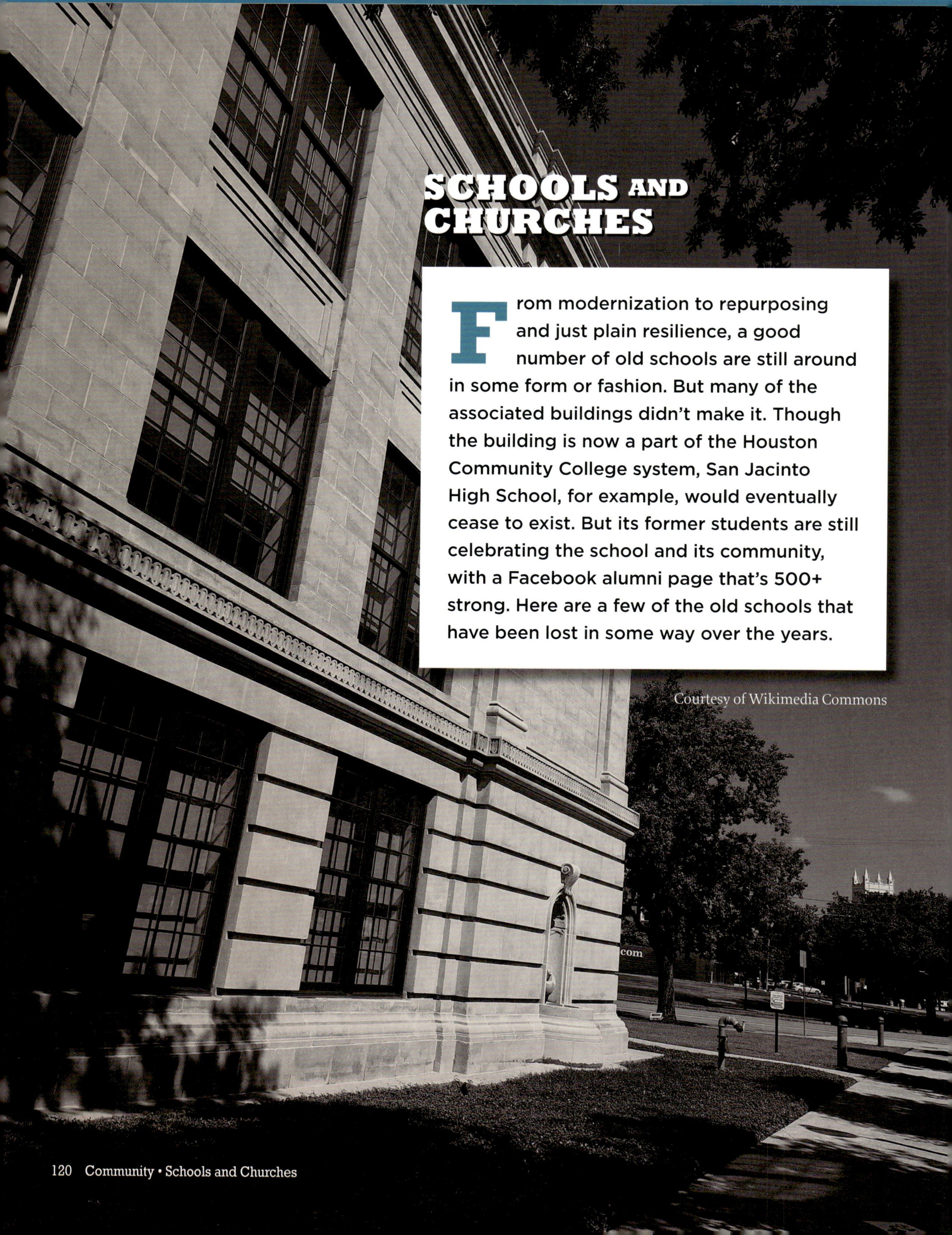

SCHOOLS AND CHURCHES

From modernization to repurposing and just plain resilience, a good number of old schools are still around in some form or fashion. But many of the associated buildings didn't make it. Though the building is now a part of the Houston Community College system, San Jacinto High School, for example, would eventually cease to exist. But its former students are still celebrating the school and its community, with a Facebook alumni page that's 500+ strong. Here are a few of the old schools that have been lost in some way over the years.

Courtesy of Wikimedia Commons

San Jacinto High School

San Jacinto High School opened in 1926 at 1300 Holman in Midtown. The columned classical revival building had 20 classrooms, a gym, and a number of upgrades and additions over the years. Notable San Jac alums include Howard Hughes, Walter Cronkite, and Denton Cooley. The school also had a significant Jewish presence in its day, with Beth Israel right around the corner. The University of Houston, originally called Houston Junior College, started in this building in 1937 before moving to its current campus in 1939. San Jac's final class was 1970; today the building is part of Houston City College.

Courtesy of University of Houston Libraries

Our Mother of Mercy School

Founded in 1928 by Louisiana Creoles who wanted their own house of worship in Houston, the Our Mother of Mercy Catholic Church opened in 1928 to serve Frenchtown in Houston's Fifth Ward. In the fall of 1930, the associated Our Mother of Mercy Catholic School was established at 2010 Benson Street to provide high-quality education to the children of the Fifth Ward at a time when segregation limited the access of black students to good schools. Initial instruction was provided by the Sisters of the Holy Family, who were based in New Orleans. Eventually the school was consolidated with St. Francis of Assisi and closed in 2020.

Courtesy of Wikimedia Commons

ARCHITECTURE AND BUILDINGS

Houston real estate development moves fast. This section could have been a whole other book. Actually it has been—my book *Lost Houston* for one, as well as *Houston Lost and Unbuilt* by Steven R. Strom, among others. Many lost Houston buildings came down to sheer growth, discarded like a crab molting as it grows on its way to 7.2 million people. The old courthouses and market squares. City Auditorium. Jeff Davis Hospital. Sometimes buildings simply reach their limit. Other times Houstonians are just ready to take the money and run. Check out these lost architectural treasures from Houston's past.

Courtesy of Jim Evans via Wikimedia Commons https://creativecommons.org/licenses/by-sa/4.0/deed.en

City Hall and Market Buildings

The square bound by Travis, Congress, Milam, and Preston was once home to a series of thriving market houses. Beginning in 1840, people brought produce, fish, and other goods to sell at the square. Eventually a city hall was added, along with banking and postal services. There was a saloon nearby. A trip to the old market square was one-stop shopping for 100+ years as four City Hall and Market House complexes were built on the site, one after the other. The last burned in 1960. Today the site is Market Square Park.

Courtesy of University of Houston Libraries

Allen Paul House

Built around 1901, many people called the Allen Paul House at 2201 Fannin the "Witch's Hat" house because of its distinctive Queen Anne style Victorian cupola. It's also known as the Hallie Pritchard House because at one point it served as the popular Hallie Pritchard School of Dance. The home was also a boarding house and a law office at various times. The Allen Paul House was designed by George Dickey, who built a number of high-profile buildings in the late 1800s—including the Sweeney, Coombs, and Fredericks Building on Main Street. After the home's 1997 demolition, the cupola was repurposed as a big, pointy park gazebo.

Courtesy of Texas Historical Comission

Texas Christian Sanitarium

Courtesy of HHRC

In the 1800s and early 1900s, sanitariums were all the rage. Primarily used to treat long-term illnesses such as tuberculosis, these healing facilities were a bit like modern hospitals. Only instead of sleepless nights with nurses and beeping waking you up, imperious medical staff, sketchy food, and staggering, unpredictable bills, the approach was to give patients lots of rest, good nutrition, fresh air, holistic treatments, and a complete lack of stress. The Texas Christian Sanitarium at 341 West 19th Street was originally a hotel that was repurposed into a sanitarium. For a time, the facility was known as the Horne Sanitarium, under Dr. J. Alvin Horne. It burned in 1915.

The Original St. Joseph's Infirmary

Houston's first major general hospital, St. Joseph's Infirmary was built in 1887 at the corner of Pierce and Crawford Streets by six Sisters of the Incarnate Word who came from Galveston. The original building was a modest wooden affair, but it was soon replaced by a better brick building that was destroyed by fire in 1894. A new red brick structure was built in 1905, but that too would be lost in time. While the old, original St. Joseph's Infirmary is long gone, a series of St. Joseph's medical facilities occupies the land to this day.

Courtesy of HHRC

The Original Binz Building

At six stories, the original Binz Building at 1001 Texas Avenue is said to have been Houston's first skyscraper. Built in 1895 across from the Capitol Hotel, it was the brainchild of German immigrant Jacob Binz, who hired Swedish architect Olle J. Lorehn to design the building. It was the first Houston building to be featured in an architectural journal; riding the elevator "all the way to the top" was a big deal for visitors. The Elks met on the top floor and must have felt like royalty. It was demolished in 1951. There is still a 13-story Binz Building at 1001 Texas Avenue today; it's the third building on that spot to have simply kept the name.

Courtesy of HHRC

Courtesy of HHRC

City Auditorium

Completed in 1910, City Auditorium at Texas and Louisiana Streets downtown was designed by Mauran & Russell architects of St. Louis. Formally known as the Houston Municipal Auditorium, generations of Houstonians got dressed up to see some of the hottest performers of the day put on shows at the auditorium ranging from Enrico Caruso to Johnny Cash, the symphony to pro wrestling. Designed in a flat and rather conservative Beaux-Arts style, it was destined to be here for a good time but not for a long time. City Auditorium was demolished in 1963, replaced by Jones Hall in 1966.

Union Station (1911)

Opening in 1911, Union Station at 501 Crawford Street was the largest Southwestern terminal station. Business travelers, soldiers returning from war, young people going off to college; everyone went through Union Station. Famous trains such as the Texas Eagle and the Sam Houston Zephyr offered service. But between commercial aviation and highway development, Union Station would close in 1974. In 1996 funds were approved to perform a historical redevelopment of the facility into a baseball stadium. Originally Enron Field, then Minute Maid Park, today's Daikin Park is built around the original lobby and other bits of Union Station. So it's not lost, but you can no longer walk in and expect to get places from there—except maybe the World Series.

Courtesy of Jerome H Farber

Courtesy of Burlington and Rock Island Railroads

Old Co-Cathedral of the Sacred Heart

This beautiful Gothic Revival building at 1111 Pierce Street was opened in 1911 to serve Houston's Irish Catholic population. Designed by Swedish-born architect Olle J. Lorehn, the church was designated a co-cathedral in the 1950s by the Archdiocese of Galveston-Houston. The Catholic church saw remarkable growth in Houston after the building's construction, so by 2008 it had to be abandoned in favor of a new $49 million facility at 1111 St. Joseph Parkway. The old Pierce Street church eventually fell prey to various and sundry wandering downtown sinners and was demolished in 2023.

Courtesy of Anthony 22

Jefferson Davis Hospital

Courtesy of HHRC

Developers of this public health facility named it after the Confederate president to make up for the fact that they built the Elder Street facility directly on top of the graves of fallen soldiers *Poltergeist*-style. I'm not saying the building, now Elder Street Artist Lofts, is haunted. But I've never been there after dark. In 1938 the hospital moved to what is today Allen Parkway. The newer moderne-style building could hold 500 patients originally. Still, Houston's relentless growth meant the facility would always struggle to keep up. The new Jeff Davis building was closed in 1989 and demolished in 1999.

Sam Houston Coliseum

Courtesy of HHRC

From the time it opened in 1937, the Sam Houston Coliseum and adjoining Houston Music Hall brought world-class live entertainment to the area. It was designed by Alfred C. Finn, and its developers mostly had the rodeo in mind. But the venue ended up hosting practically every popular musical act of its day, including the Beatles, the Rolling Stones, the Doors, Genesis, Lynyrd Skynyrd, Queen, Elton John, Led Zeppelin, and more. It was also the home of Houston Pro Wrestling. "No, not the Iron Claw! Ahhh!" Both buildings were demolished in 1998 to make way for the Hobby Center for the Performing Arts.

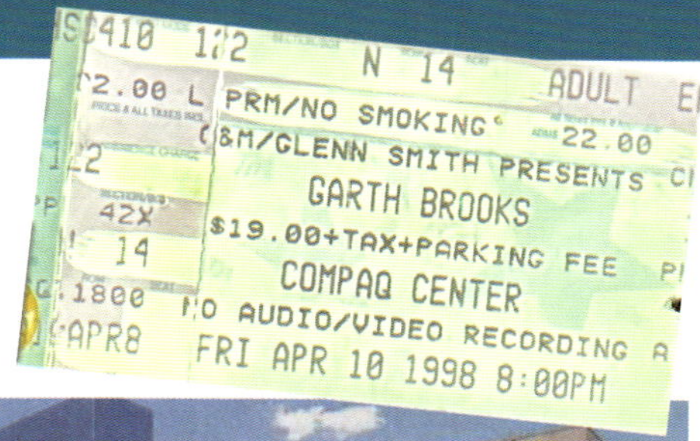

The Summit/Compaq Center

Hosting its first performance in 1975, the Summit at 3700 Southwest Freeway would follow the Houston Coliseum as the city's go-to concert venue. It had a capacity of around 17,000. The Who was the first band to play the venue; everyone from Stevie Ray Vaughan to Billy Joel would follow. It became the Compaq Center in 1998, the first Houston sports venue to sell naming rights. Aside from concerts, it also served as the home of Houston Rockets/Comets basketball as well as pro ice skating, tennis matches, circuses, comedy, arena football, and more. The Compaq Center became home to Joel Osteen's Lakewood Church in 2005. Lakewood is the most "mega" of all the Houston megachurches.

Courtesy of Gemini 7

Courtesy of Boston Public Library

The Prudential Building

Post-WWII, Prudential Insurance sought to grow in major cities around the country and lock down market share. So the Prudential Insurance Company Building in the 1100 block of Holcombe Boulevard that opened in 1952 was part of that big push. At 18 stories, it made a statement. The mid-century-modern building also offered amenities that included an outdoor swimming pool and tennis courts. Strategically located in the Texas Medical Center, it no doubt gave the business a leg up in the growing Houston metro. But progress spares few, even on the executive fast track. MD Anderson bought the building in 1974; it was demolished in 2012.

Courtesy of HHRC

Preston Avenue Farmers Market

In 1929 a new 100,000+ square foot farmers market building was erected at Preston Avenue, jutting out over Buffalo Bayou. Market Square had gotten unbearably crowded, and this would be a more organized way for farmers to sell their goods. The facility offered almost 300 vendor stalls, which must have beat sitting in your truck in the Texas sun. The Preston Avenue Farmers Market offered restrooms, free parking, and even a restaurant. But by the late 1950s, the facility was demolished as the modern grocery store lured customers with convenience. Today the Wortham Theater Center sits on the property.

ICONS AND CURIOSITIES

For my money, these quirky outliers were some of Houston's most interesting lost treasures. Big cities are feeling more and more the same these days. But does every big city have a train that goes to the beach every 45 minutes? Do they all have a free catalog you can pick up at any bar or restaurant and sign up for an Asian cooking class or car maintenance course on the cheap? An actual functioning space shuttle? A random button that burps a nearby bayou? Well, Houston doesn't have any of that stuff either. But we did, and here are their stories.

Courtesy of HHRC

Early Light Rail

Most Houstonians don't give our underwhelming modern light rail, circa 2004, much thought unless you live downtown or near the Texas Medical Center. But way back in 1927, the peak of early electric railcars in H-Town, Houston had a massive rail system with 24 routes and 90 miles of track. Electric rail cars connected practically every sizable real estate development and commercial center in town. In fact, the electric rail company was one of Houston's largest employers. But the rise of the automobile, economic pressures, suburban development, and other factors would mean that the last of the old electric streetcars were shut down in the summer of 1940.

Courtesy of HHRC

Turnverein

Turnverein was a German movement founded in the 1880s that emphasized physical fitness, community engagement, and cultural activities for the German people. Turnvereins were like little gymnastic societies where "Turners" could work out, bowl, and spend time with fellow Deutschfolk. The first Houston Turnverein building was on Caroline Street, but the most beautiful was its replacement: a lovely Art Deco building designed by Joseph Finger in the 1920s at Southmore and Almeda. Sadly, it was demolished in 1993. At one time, there were almost 30 of these clubs in Texas; believe it or not the Turnverein in Boerne, Texas, is still going strong. *Prost!*

Courtesy of HHRC

Houston Light Guard

In the late 1800s and early 1900s, it was normal for communities to have a militia composed of everyday citizens whom you could call when you needed men with guns to do men-with-guns stuff. The Houston Light Guard was the first such organization activated in Houston after the War Between the States. Chartered in 1873, the unit participated in—and often won—drill competitions between deployments. They put their personal lives on hold to fight in the Spanish-American War and both World Wars. The Houston Light Guard was deactivated after WWII but reorganized twice during the Vietnam War. Thank you for your service, gentlemen, wherever you are.

Courtesy of HHRC

Galveston-Houston Electric Railway

From 1911 to 1936, you could catch a train every hour between Houston and Galveston. Spearheaded by a group of Houston investors, the Galveston-Houston Electric Railway made it so convenient to catch a train between Houston and Galveston that people could live that island life and commute into Houston for work—no car required. From six in the morning until eleven at night, 18 cars went each way. With 50.7 miles of rail length, including the newly built Galveston Causeway, it was designed by Boston engineering company Stone & Webster and powered by a dedicated power plant near Webster, Texas. The rise of the automobile and shifting economics mean you've got to find your own way to the beach these days.

Courtesy of University of Houston Libraries

Camp Logan

Courtesy of US War Dept

Before the jogging and bike trails, tennis courts, and PGA golf, the land that is now Memorial Park served as a World War I training camp called Camp Logan. One of 16 National Guard camps commissioned to spin up the American military machine for WWI, Camp Logan was a huge facility, practically a small town. Actually, not even that small—just a proper town. Troops stationed there underwent basic training, practiced drills and marksmanship, performed field exercises, received specialized courses, and prepped for overseas deployment. At the close of the war the prominent Hogg family acquired the site and turned 1,000 acres over to the City of Houston for use as a park because they were cool like that.

Courtesy of Boston Public Library

The Original Camp Strake

Oilman George William Strake (1894–1969) served on the national executive board of the Boy Scouts of America, donating the land that would become Camp Strake. Just south of Conroe and to the west of Interstate 45, Camp Strake's 2,175 acres were home to generations of Scouts as they visited the camp to earn merit badges, attend special events, hike, swim, shoot, and just enjoy the great outdoors. But the area, and Texas in general, changed quite a bit after Camp Strake's 1944 opening. When the concrete and city lights got too close, the old camp closed in 2014 and moved to a new location.

Proposed Monorail

Hey, you know that cool, space-age monorail all Houstonians get to enjoy these days? Of course you don't because it, too, was lost. The inventor of the modern monorail system was Houston entrepreneur Murel Goodell. His prototype, the Trailblazer, was tested at Houston's Arrowhead Park in 1956. The event made quite the splash; Roy Rogers and his horse, Trigger, were in attendance. In the long run, though, city planners couldn't stomach the price of the futuristic-looking rail system. Goodell went on to build several more, however, including the famous Disneyland monorail, but the Trailblazer was dismantled in 1964—eventually converted into an East Texas home.

Courtesy of HHRC

Courtesy of HHRC

The Gulf Building "Lollipop" Sign

In 1966 the installation of a 58-foot rotating Gulf Oil Co. sign composed of blue letters on a fat, orange disk was completed atop the Art Deco Gulf Building at Main Street and Rusk Avenue. Most thought of it as "the lollipop." Some people thought of it as the worst thing to happen to Houston since the Spanish flu. Love it or hate it, though, you couldn't miss it—it was the world's largest rotating sign at the time with 7,000+ feet of neon tubing. Those who thought the lollipop a garish eyesore won the day in 1973, and the sign came down.

Kitirik

It's unlikely your guidance counselor suggested donning a leotard and dressing like a black cat for television audiences, but it worked out great for the lovely Bunny Orsak. The KTRK Channel 13 mascot hosted a popular local daily children's TV show from 1954 to 1971. Her mother made the costume's hat. Orsak had special guests, celebrated kids' birthdays, and just brightened up the Houston air waves in general. A contest was held to name the black cat character—because of "unlucky" Channel 13—and the winner had simply inserted the letter "i" between the call letters of the TV station to create a "kiti" cat.

Courtesy of Natalie Bond

Leisure Learning Unlimited

Cooking. Do-it-yourself. Photography. For more than 30 years, if you were an adult who liked learning new things, you were probably a fan of Leisure Learning Unlimited. Founded by Ted Weisgal and Kathy Kamin, LLU used to print little booklets of available classes and distribute them around town to restaurants, stores, and bars. You'd just pick up a course catalogue, thumb through it, register, and *boom* you had something cool to do. And you'd always meet the most interesting people. But with the proliferation of global online courses, and other factors, class was dismissed for Leisure Learning Unlimited in 2017.

Courtesy of Kampus Productions

The Big Bubble

Along the Preston Street bridge you'll find a red button. No sign. No instructions. No clue as to what it does. Just a red button begging people to push it. At one time, if you mashed this mysterious button, an enormous bubble would erupt from the murky waters of nearby Buffalo Bayou. "Burping the bayou" was part of a Dean Ruck art installation that had the ecological purpose of randomly oxygenating the at-times-stagnant bayou water. It was a fun, quirky concept that supported the health of this prominent Houston waterway. Sadly, the Big Bubble was destroyed during Hurricane Harvey, and the City of Houston has other things to worry about these days.

The Space Shuttle Program

There were five functional space shuttles: *Challenger*, *Endeavor*, *Discovery*, *Atlantis*, and *Columbia*. A sixth, *Enterprise*, was a prototype used for glide testing. NASA's Lyndon B. Johnson Space Center in Houston was home to the space shuttle program from 1981 to 2011. Altogether, Houston supported these spacecraft through 135 missions that included launching the Hubble Space Telescope. You'd think the surviving shuttles would be on display at Space Center Houston—or at least *somewhere* in Houston. But after the program spun down, Houston's last shuttle, *Endeavor*, was flown off to Los Angeles for eventual display in the California Science Center. Now only a replica is on site at JSC.

Courtesy of Library of Congress

The Original "Garage Mahal"

Houston's Art Car Museum at 140 Heights Boulevard was founded in 1998 by prominent Houston artist and collector Ann Harithas. I loved this quirky little place. A nonprofit, the space housed not only a number of mobile media works but also all kinds of interesting contemporary art. After the passing of Harithas and her husband, James, the museum was left to their son and daughters. The doors closed at the original Art Car Museum in March 2024, but plans and funding are already in place to give the works housed in the museum a new home in the future.

Courtesy of Don Seributra

INDUSTRY

Industry is what Houston does. According to the *Financial Times*, Houston leads US cities in terms of exports (ahead of New York) and was ranked as the top US city for foreign investment. And we're not bad at crawfish, either. Of course, big business takes big risks, and this section could've been its own book. I included Enron, though I realize it might not seem like much of a treasure to many. But if you knew people who worked there, or worked there yourself, you know that while it ended badly it started brilliantly and with a ton of talented people. Let's see what other industrial empires can no longer be found around town.

Courtesy of WhispertoMe

Enron

Founded in 1985 with the merger of two natural gas companies, Enron went beyond utilities to pioneer the energy derivative. At one point Enron had a stock price of $90+ and was number seven in the Fortune 500. It recruited the best business minds of its day. Over its skis with debt, however, even the most creative accounting couldn't save it, and the company's downfall was legendary. In the rest of the country, Enron was some abstract cultural event or concept of modern corporate chicanery. But, of course, a lot of Houstonians worked there and wound up carrying a cardboard box out of 1400 Smith Street. There's nothing abstract about a day like that.

Courtesy of Enron Corporation

Stanford Financial Group

There was actually a time when the now-defunct Stanford Financial Group served as a Houston treasure. Though technically headquartered in Antigua (naturally), this high-flying investment firm kept a prominent Galleria office. Founder Allen Stanford himself rarely visited his Houston location, but it provided hundreds of jobs for Houstonians. Mexia-born Stanford was known for his philanthropy, as well as for living a lavish lifestyle. Unfortunately, not all of the money was his to spend. In 2012, Stanford was sentenced to 110 years in prison for orchestrating a $7 billion investment fraud scheme.

Compaq Computer Corporation

In the early 1980s, Texas Instruments was a leader in semiconductors, electronics, and consumer products. Three ambitious Texas Instruments employees broke away from the company in 1982 to form their own enterprise: the Compaq Computer Corporation. The company's first portable—well, lug-able, really—was wildly successful despite weighing almost 30 pounds. These computers were actually some of the first to run IBM software. Compaq would go on to become a best-selling computer brand in the 1980s and 1990s. In 1999 it was the world's fourth-largest IT company. It merged with Hewlett-Packard in 2002, which eventually phased out the brand and left the Houston area with one less big-name tech company.

Courtesy of Brian R. Lueck

The Original Gulf Oil

Gulf Oil dates back to the 1901 Spindletop oil field. Originally called the Guffey Company, it had a number of investors, including the Mellon family of Pennsylvania. The group also started a refining company in Port Arthur, as well as a network of pipelines. Eventually the company expanded internationally. Gulf created the first drive-in gas station and sponsored a legacy of high-end European racing cars. By the early 1980s, Gulf was the sixth-largest US oil company. Gulf was sold to Chevron in 1984 for $13.2 billion—the largest corporate merger up to that point. After the Chevron merger, the Gulf name no longer accompanied operations like exploration or refining, but Atlanta retailer RaceTrac owns the brand for retail purposes.

Courtesy of Robert Yarnall Richie

Brown Shipbuilding Company

During WWII, the nation thirsted for ships as a means of imposing American military will, enabling supply chains, and controlling key waterways for the Allied powers. Founded in Houston, Brown & Root (today KBR) has a legacy in construction going back to 1919. When the fight was on, the firm stepped up to start this subsidiary to fuel the war effort. Brown Shipbuilding Company cranked out 350+ vessels during WWII. Brown & Root sold the yard to the Todd Houston Shipbuilding Company, which closed in the 1980s. Brown & Root picked the facility up once again for barge construction and repair. In 2004, the property was sold piecemeal to a number of buyers and is now known as Brown Shipbuilding Industrial Park.

Courtesy of HHRC

Anderson, Clayton & Company

Courtesy of Library of Congress

At one time cotton was big business in Houston. In the late 1800s, we even had the Houston Cotton Exchange Board of Trade, a sort of Wall Street-like center-of-gravity for the regional industry. Moving to town in 1916, the successful cotton merchants at Anderson, Clayton & Company of Houston had more than just business savvy; they had ambition. After two world wars, some clever boxing, and impressive overseas business development skills, this company became the world's largest buyer, seller, and shipper of raw cotton by 1945. As the 20th century progressed, however, the business would mostly transition to food processing and sell to Quaker Oats in 1986.

Continental Airlines

Courtesy of André DuPont

Founded in 1934 as Varney Airlines, Continental was for decades synonymous with dependable, comfortable air travel. Even in the Spartan and psychopathic modern airline industry, Continental was one of the carriers least likely to demand a normal-sized human to sit in an esoteric yoga position. The airline moved its headquarters to Houston from Los Angeles in 1983 following a hostile takeover by Texas Air. George Bush Intercontinental Airport (IAH) would become a major hub. Continental created jobs, facilitated investment in the airport, and made it easier to reach much of the world from H-Town. It merged with United Airlines in 2012.

Transco Energy Company

When long-time Houstonians refer to the Williams Tower as the Transco Tower, they're referring to Houston's former Transco Energy Company. Its main business was the transportation and sale of natural gas. Representing an astonishing network of pipelines spanning more than 10,000 miles running from South Texas to New York City, the Transco pipelines moved around 15 percent of all US natural gas. When constructed in 1949, it was the longest pipeline in the world. While Transco's pipelines are still in play, the Transco Energy Company brand disappeared when the company was acquired by Tulsa-based Williams Energy in 1995.

Courtesy of Bill Jacobus

Houston Lighting & Power

The original Houston Electric Light & Power Company was founded in 1882. The company charged a flat rate for all customers, and soon went flat broke. The company changed hands a few times before becoming Houston Lighting and Power Company in 1901, the brand 20th century Houstonians would associate with their power bill for almost an entire century. The company was renamed Reliant Energy in 1999, and then split into three different companies in 2003: Reliant Energy, CenterPoint Energy, and Texas Genco (now NRG). The breakup came as a result of retail deregulation efforts that demanded separation of operating functions.

Courtesy of Patrick Feller

{COMMUNITY}

NEIGHBORHOODS

As permanent as they feel, not all neighborhoods stand the test of time. When neighborhoods go away or move here in Houston, it's usually one of two things: money or Mother Nature. Gentrification reshuffles the deck everywhere you find it, as when the original Little Saigon in Midtown was redeveloped into everything from trendy condos and apartments to urban park space. Of course, hurricanes and flooding have taken out more than a few lovely Houston neighborhoods. Fortunately, the friendships we make within these communities can last longer than the homes and buildings. Let's look back at some of Houston's lost neighborhoods.

Courtesy of historicimages-store

Courtesy of HHRC

Harrisburg

Only a lawsuit involving the estate of the late New York entrepreneur John Harris kept Harrisburg from being named the capital of the Republic of Texas in 1836, rather than Houston. Just south of where the Brays and Buffalo Bayous meet, this old trading post recovered nicely from being burned to the ground by General Santa Anna during the Texas Revolution. Its location on the Houston Ship Channel was both a blessing and a curse, but in 1926 the town ceased to exist when annexed by the City of Houston. A state historical marker at 1001 Broadway Street commemorates Old Harrisburg.

The Original Chinatown

Before it was branded as EaDo and sported soccer, murals, and craft beer-laden Thursday night happy hours for people who probably have to get up and go to work in the morning, the eastern edge of downtown was Houston's original Chinatown. The area sported the three-story On Leong Chinese Merchants Association building at 801 Chartres (1951), a Chinese school, churches, community hubs, apartments, and Chinese American businesses ranging from bakeries to law firms. There were factories that made noodles and egg rolls, and stores like the Kim Hung Supermarket offered authentic imported Chinese groceries and home goods. In the 1980s, however, waves of development began pushing Chinese businesses westward out to Bellaire Boulevard and the Asiatown Houstonians know today.

Courtesy of WispertoMe

Midtown's Little Saigon

After the fall of Saigon, Houston took in a number of Vietnamese immigrants. Many wound up in Midtown, establishing a thriving Little Saigon that would last for decades. Midtown had a strong Little Saigon brand complete with Vietnamese street signs and official recognition from the City of Houston as the hub of the Vietnamese community. But the 1990s began patterns of development and gentrification that drove many in the Vietnamese community farther west to the Bellaire Boulevard area. And while Houston's Vietnamese community continues to thrive, the old Little Saigon in Midtown is largely lost. (Thankfully, Mai's lives on post-fire).

Courtesy of WhispertoMe

Arbor Oaks

Developed in the early 1970s, Arbor Oaks was a perfectly lovely subdivision in Northwest Houston. It offered quiet suburban living with modern ranch-style homes that middle-class Houstonians could afford. Unfortunately, it also sat at the confluence of White Oak Bayou and Vogel Creek. Eventually, the low-lying area became heavily developed without much natural drainage or engineered flood mitigation. Homes in the neighborhood flooded with practically every bad storm. After Tropical Storm Allison in 2001, residents began selling their homes to the county. By the time Hurricane Harvey rolled around, there were only 13 homes left in the neighborhood. Each one flooded. Today no homes remain.

EVENTS

Good times never last, it seems, and when a big, city-wide event goes away it leaves a hole in the calendars of a whole community. Way back in the day, practically the entire city of Houston took the week off for No-Tsu-Oh, a citywide Mardi Gras–like celebration. There were extravagant parades and balls, as well as college football; Texas A&M University and the University of Texas at Austin played well-attended games at No-Tsu-Oh for a few years. Starting in the early 1930s, the Texas Prison Rodeo hung on for more than 50 years—drawing 100,000 attendees at its peak. Check out these treasured events from yesterday's H-Town.

Courtesy of Ed Schipul

Courtesy of HHRC

No-Tsu-Oh

For years early Houstonians looked to the lavish Mardi Gras festivals of New Orleans with envy. So in 1899, they decided to do something about it. Enter No-Tsu-Oh. While it wouldn't have the religious component of Mardi Gras, it would celebrate something always close to Houston's heart: capitalism. Touting the city as a hub of industry, No-Tsu-Oh (Houston backward) elected kings such as King Nottoc (Cotton), Retaw (Water), etc. Tens of thousands of people flocked into town for a week of costume balls, carnivals, college football, and drunken debauchery. Honestly, it sounds pretty awesome. But the annual party ended for good when WWI rolled around and Houstonians had more important things to invest their money in than earning a county-wide hangover.

The Texas Prison Rodeo

From 1931 to 1986, the Texas Prison Rodeo was held at a baseball park outside the Walls Unit in Huntsville—about an hour north of Houston. The rodeo offered a number of events, such as bull riding, calf roping, and "Convict Poker," whereby a bull was released while convicts sat at a poker table. Jeez, the *huevos* on these guys. The rodeo also hosted concerts featuring country music greats like Willie Nelson, Loretta Lynn, George Strait, and of course, Johnny Cash. The Texas Prison Rodeo was even featured in the 1980 film *Urban Cowboy*. But concerns over liability, finances, and the deteriorating stadium meant lights out in 1986.

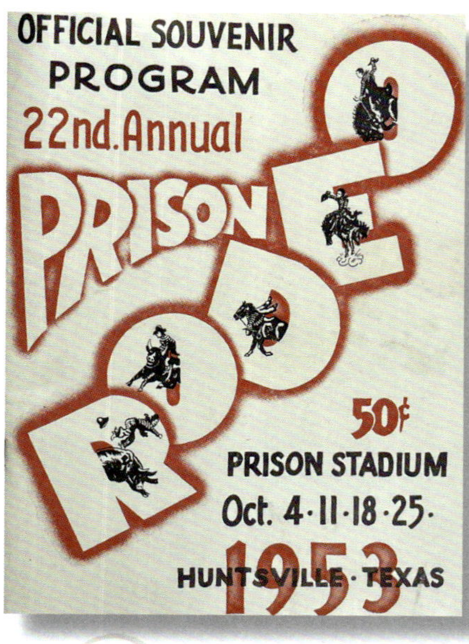

Original Houston Moonlight Ramble

For decades it wasn't unusual to see an armada of cyclists, some in Halloween costumes, perhaps with questionable sobriety, blow by your house at 2 a.m. The Moonlight Ramble was a nighttime cycling race started in the early 1970s and inspired by a similar event in St. Louis. Founded by Daniel and Joy Boone, who ran a popular cycle shop for decades, the Moonlight Ramble became an annual tradition for many Houstonians. A number of financial, safety, and logistical challenges drove it to eventually roll up into the spring Art Bike parade. But by 2024 there was no sign of the event, moonlit or otherwise.

Courtesy of Flo Maderebner

Houstoncon

Houstoncon was a comic book, sci-fi, and pop culture fan convention first held in 1967 where many culturally significant movements are often born: a Ramada Inn at Interstate 45 and the Allen Parkway. Over the years the event picked up momentum, reorganized, and migrated to bigger and bigger venues. Programs showcased original comic book–inspired artwork, and fans flocked to see some of their favorite actors, writers, artists, and creators. In 1974 and 1975 it was combined in a Vulcan mind-meld kind of way with the local Star Trek con. The final event in 1982 was apparently a disaster jokingly referred to as "The Con of Wrath."

The Texaco Grand Prix of Houston

From 1998 to 2001, a section of downtown Houston in front of the George R. Brown was transformed into a racetrack. A part of the now-defunct Championship Auto Racing Team (CART) organization, the Grand Prix of Houston raced open-wheel vehicles most people call "Indy cars." They're similar to Formula One cars, though not quite as advanced. The race demanded 100 laps around the approximately 1.5-mile course, though rain washed out the premiere event at the 70-lap mark. Races returned in 2006/2007 and 2013/2014, but the original downtown venue that energized the city never came back.

PEOPLE

From the jet set to the streets, Houston has been home to many who've left a legacy. The name Hughes starts conversations to this day, as many Hughes family business endeavors are still going strong in some form or other. We'll get to the Menil family's art patronage, but nobody ever talks about how John de Menil was a war hero. He received the *Croix de Guerre* from the French government for his role in sabotaging oil shipments that were bound for Nazi Germany. Here are just a few people of many who count as true lost treasures of Houston.

Courtesy of Library of Congress

Howard Hughes Jr. (1905–1976)

The son of a famous oilfield inventor—and arguably the bigger treasure of the two—Howard Hughes Jr. was a man of adventure. He broke the land speed record, dated Hollywood starlets, flew around the world in less than four days, made movies, explored the Arctic, and even collaborated with the CIA to help recover a sunken Soviet submarine. He also broke almost every bone in his body when he crashed an experimental photo reconnaissance airplane into a Beverly Hills neighborhood. He had long, high-profile battles with both mental illness and Las Vegas real estate. Hughes died on an airplane headed back to Houston and is buried at Glenwood Cemetery.

Courtesy of Wikimedia Commons

John de Menil (1904–1973) and Dominique de Menil (1908–1997)

This mid-century power couple is one of the reasons why Houston is today a modern art destination. John and Dominique de Menil fled Nazi-occupied France. John had been a banker before the war, president of Banque Nationale pour le Commerce et l'Industrie. Dominique's father had founded the high-tech oilfield services company Schlumberger (today SLB), which John would eventually join. The couple settled in Houston, where they would nurture their passion for collecting art. Eventually, the Menils would amass more than 16,000 paintings, sculptures, drawings, books, photographs, prints, and *objets d'art* made public in 1987 as the Menil Collection.

Courtesy of WhispertoMe

Dr. Michael DeBakey (1908–2008)

A native of Lake Charles, Dr. Michael DeBakey moved to Houston in 1948 to serve as the head of the surgical department at the Baylor University College of Medicine. He'd spend decades innovating there—eventually serving as CEO, president, and a number of other prestigious roles. He performed an astounding 60,000+ surgeries in his lifetime. A renowned cardiovascular surgeon and medical pioneer, his list of firsts, accomplishments, and technical developments was heroic, among them performing the first successful coronary bypass operation and being the first person to successfully implant a left ventricular bypass pump. He's buried in Arlington National Cemetery.

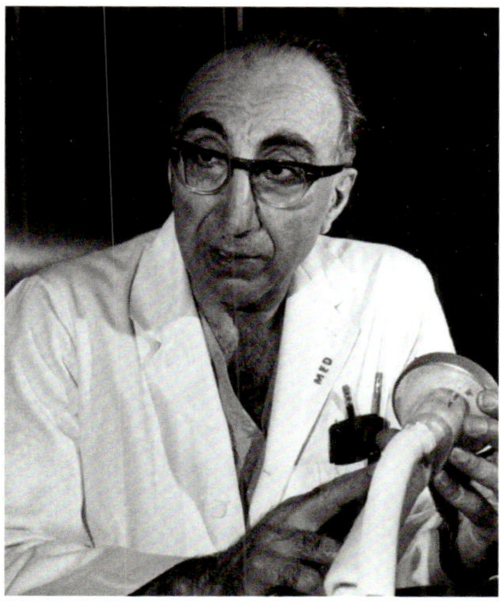

Courtesy of University of Houston Digital Library

George H. W. Bush (1924–2018)

George Herbert Walker Bush, who would become the 41st president of the United States, moved to Houston in 1958 as an oil and gas executive. In 1963 he became chairman of the Harris County Republican Party. He served two terms as a District 7 Congressman, launching an iconic public service career including not just the presidency but also running the Central Intelligence Agency. From the eight-foot bronze statue in Sesquicentennial Park to IAH Airport and the George H. W. Bush Presidential Library and Museum up the road in College Station, the legacy of the elder Bush can still be found all over town. Fun fact: Bush Sr. had an impressive collection of fun dress socks—always wearing the perfect pair for any occasion. A former naval aviator, he was laid to rest in a pair of socks sporting fighter planes.

Courtesy of David Valdez

Barbara Bush (1925–2018)

She met her husband-to-be at a Christmas dance—moving to town with him in the late 1950s. Bush worked tirelessly over the years to support her husband's career while managing her five children. Second Lady in 1981 and First Lady in 1989, she was also mother of 43rd president George W. Bush and 43rd governor of Florida Jeb Bush. Her philanthropic works in Houston were countless, supporting organizations such as MD Anderson Cancer Center, Texas Children's Hospital, and the Houston Public Library system. But she's most well-known for the Barbara Bush Foundation for Family Literacy, founded in 2013, which strives to improve Houston literacy rates to this day. She was the only American woman who saw both her husband and son take the presidential oath of office.

Courtesy of the White House

Dr. Red Duke (1928–2015)

Ennis-born James "Red" Duke was a renowned trauma surgeon and healthcare advocate who made a lasting impact on the medical community in Houston. The man was a force of nature in the surgical theater. Childhood friends with Willie Nelson, he listened to country music as he operated. Dr. Duke had a syndicated TV segment promoting good health, after which he'd sign off, "from the University of Texas Health Science Center at Houston, I'm Dr. Red Duke." He also started Memorial Hermann's Life Flight program, which has saved countless lives in the region. He died in 2015 at the age of 86.

Courtesy of Texas Medical Center

"Dusty" Hill (1949–2021)

With its Southern blues-rock sound, ZZ Top is legendary in these parts—and Joseph Michael "Dusty" Hill was its original bass guitarist. Born in Dallas, Hill began playing with his brother, also a musician. By the time he was 20 years old Dusty was a sideman for blues superstar Lightnin' Hopkins. In 1970 he joined ZZ Top, which he helped make a Texas icon for 50+ years. Both he and singer/guitarist Billy Gibbons were known for their long, flowing beards; ironically, the third member of the band, Frank Beard, was clean shaven. Despite his talent and success, Hill was known for his humility and easygoing personality. He died in his sleep here in Houston. Rest in peace, Dusty—you were one of Texas's greatest hits.

Courtesy of Ralph Arvesen

Patrick Swayze (1952–2009)

Swayze grew up in Houston's Oak Forest neighborhood. His mother, Patsy, owned a dance studio—first in Bellaire and later in the Heights. Swayze broke out as Prince Charming in *Disney on Parade*, starred as Danny in a Broadway production of *Grease*, and then went on to become an A-List Hollywood actor. The *Outsiders*, *Dirty Dancing*, *Red Dawn*, *Road House*, *Ghost*, *Point Break*, *Donnie Darko*—his filmography showcases some of the most fun and iconic productions of his day. He was named Sexiest Man Alive by *People* magazine in 1991. Swayze passed away at 57 after a fight with pancreatic cancer.

DJ Screw (1971–2000)

Robert Earl Davis Jr. used mixtapes to pioneer his own music sound and raise the profile of Houston hip-hop. Davis slowed the tempo of the music—skipping, scratching, and repeating lyrics to create a unique and ethereal sound. Choosing big love over big money, he sold his music directly to fans, first at his house and then at Screwed Up Records and Tapes on Cullen Boulevard. Davis also featured other Houston artists in his mixes, the "Screwed Up Click," creating not just a genre but a scene. He died in his record studio, a result of a codeine overdose.

George Foreman (1949–2025)

"Big George" was born in Marshall but raised in Houston's Fifth Ward. It wasn't an easy childhood, and his life could have easily gone a different way. But through boxing he found his focus. Winning a gold medal at the 1968 Summer Olympics as a heavyweight, Foreman made a name for himself as a formidable fighter with tremendous power and technical skill. By the time he first stepped into the ring with Joe Frazier, he'd racked up a 37-0 record. He beat Frazier, winning the world heavyweight title. By the end of his career he'd won 76 of his 81 fights. But he wasn't just a champion in the ring; he was a champion for H-Town too. Foreman brought national attention to Houston, created a community center in the Fifth Ward, opened a local church as an ordained minister, mentored young Houstonians in boxing, and spread plenty of that grill money around town. Big George deserves big thanks.

Courtesy of Nationaal Archief Fotocollectie Anefo

PLAYERS AND COACHES

Houston has long been home to world-class athletes and coaches. Guy Lewis established a decades-long legacy in college hoops at the University of Houston. And Texas being Texas, we've had our share of football greats. Bill Yeoman built a formidable UH football program. Homespun Bum Phillips became one of the most beloved Texas football coaches ever. Known for his trademark hat, he was too much of a gentleman to wear it indoors—even in the Astrodome. Let's look at these legends.

Courtesy of Library of Congress

Guy V. Lewis (1922–2015)

Lewis was the game-changing head basketball coach at the University of Houston for 30 years, building a legacy of strong play maintained to this day—their brutal defense always cutting deep through NCAA opponents. After serving as an assistant coach, Lewis became head coach in 1956. His legacy was secured in 1968 when the Coogs slapped UCLA with an extra "L" in front of 53,000 fans at the Astrodome (Kareem Abdul-Jabbar was on the opposing team). He also anointed "Phi Slama Jama," the power team that included Hakeem Olajuwon and Clyde Drexler. He retired in 1986 and was eventually inducted into the National Collegiate Basketball Hall of Fame.

Courtesy of University of Houston

Bill Yeoman (1927–2020)

Every Texas college football franchise has coaching legends. At the University of Houston, William Frank "Bill" Yeoman is up there with the best. A West Point grad, Yeoman coached at Michigan State before landing at UH in 1962 as head coach. He led the Houston football team for an amazing 25 seasons, during which time he brought home four Southwest Conference (those were the days) championships, as well as two Cotton Bowl wins. Yeoman pioneered the Veer Offense, a triple option approach many teams would soon adopt. In 2015, a statue of Yeoman was erected at TDECU Stadium at the University of Houston's main campus.

Courtesy of University of Houston

Oail "Bum" Phillips (1923–2013)

Phillips coached the Oilers during its "Luv Ya Blue" glory days, such as they were. Born in Orange, Phillips played college ball before serving in the US Marine Corps during WWII. When he came home he coached high school and college, then got on with the Chargers. He was at Houston in 1975 until moving on to the Saints in 1981. The cowboy hat-wearing coach brought more than a 59-38 record; he brought a larger-than-life good guy persona that earned respect on and off the field. He once said, "Dallas Cowboys may be America's team, but the Houston Oilers are Texas's team."

Courtesy of AJ Guel

Carroll Dawson (1938-2024)

Courtesy of Baylor University

For almost 30 years, Alba-born Carroll Dawson helped support the home team at the Houston Rockets. Through talent, discipline, and hard work, "CD" earned a spot on the Baylor basketball team as a young man, where he was named All-Southwest Conference and Southwest Conference Outstanding Player. He went on to coach at Baylor. After joining the Rockets in 1979, he helped Rudy T. nail down back-to-back NBA titles in the mid-1990s. Dawson brought in tons of talent during his time as general manager, advocating endlessly for both the team and Houston. He was also integral in launching the WNBA's Houston Comets.

Drew Hill (1956–2011)

Courtesy of Acroterion

This legendary two-time Pro Bowler was an integral part of the Oilers' "run and shoot" offense for seven seasons between 1985 and 1991. Hill played ball at Georgia Tech before joining the Rams in 1979, then moving on to play in Houston under both Jerry Glanville and Jack Pardee. An unstoppable wide receiver with ice water in his veins, Hill made almost 500 receptions during his Houston days. After the 1991 season, Hill moved to Atlanta, where he played two years for the Falcons before suffering a stroke and passing away at just 54 years old. Luv ya, Drew.

Steve "Air" McNair (1973–2009)

Courtesy of Keith Allison

A Mississippi native, McNair served as quarterback at Alcorn State University before being drafted to the Houston Oilers in 1995 (this was a few years after the Warren Moon era). McNair was a leader on the field, smart and athletic; he was also a dual threat who could move the ball on his own when needed. He continued to play after the franchise was moved to Tennessee in 1999, eventually joining the Baltimore Ravens in 2006. In 2009, McNair was tragically murdered by his 20-year-old girlfriend, who then died by suicide. The Tennessee Titans retired McNair's No. 9 jersey in his honor.

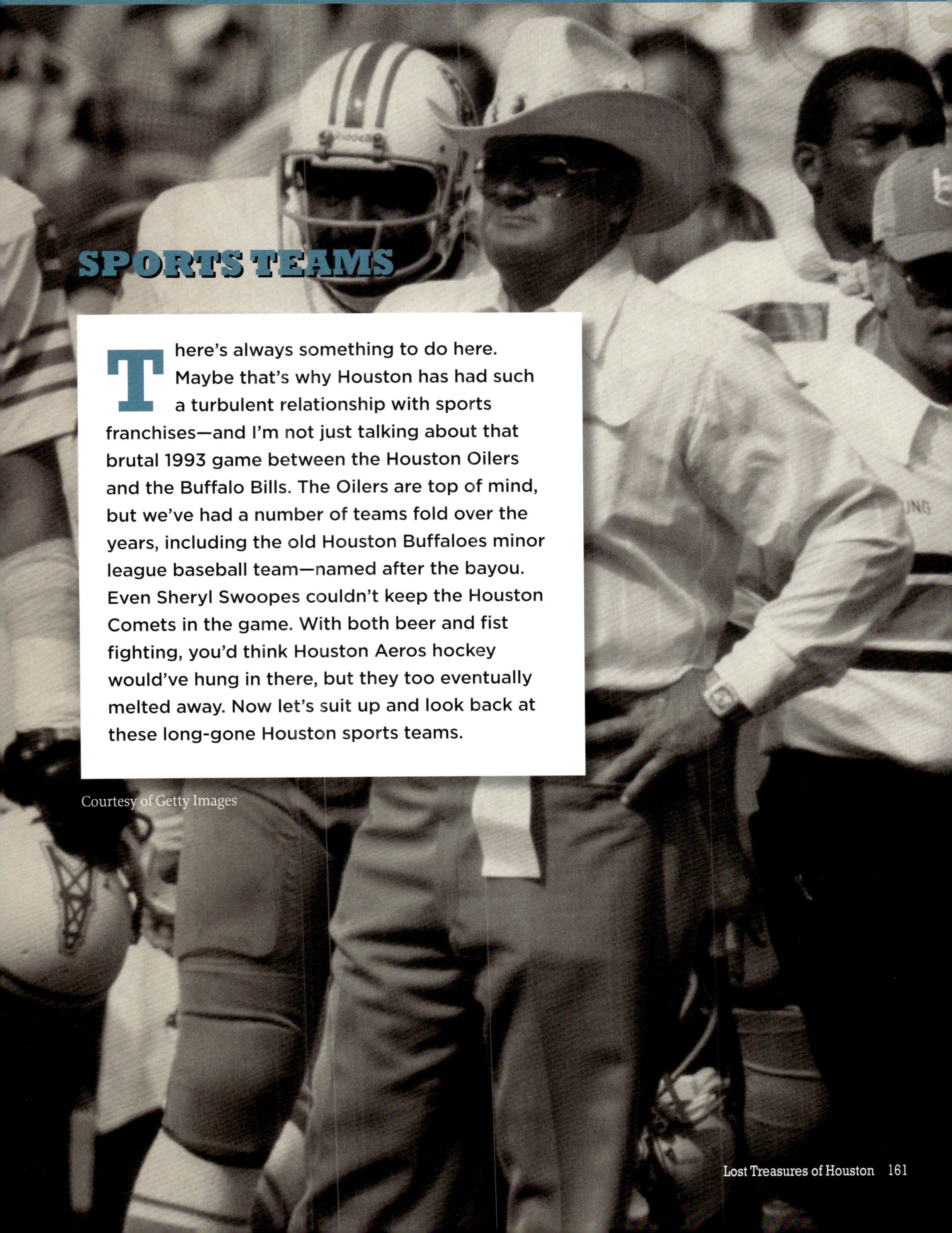

SPORTS TEAMS

There's always something to do here. Maybe that's why Houston has had such a turbulent relationship with sports franchises—and I'm not just talking about that brutal 1993 game between the Houston Oilers and the Buffalo Bills. The Oilers are top of mind, but we've had a number of teams fold over the years, including the old Houston Buffaloes minor league baseball team—named after the bayou. Even Sheryl Swoopes couldn't keep the Houston Comets in the game. With both beer and fist fighting, you'd think Houston Aeros hockey would've hung in there, but they too eventually melted away. Now let's suit up and look back at these long-gone Houston sports teams.

Courtesy of Getty Images

Houston Oilers

Born into an oil family, K. S. "Bud" Adams started both the American Football League (AFL) and the Houston Oilers football franchise. The Oilers won AFL championships in 1960 and 1961. They began playing in the Astrodome in 1968 and would go 243-283-6 between 1960 and 1995. While they sometimes fell short on the field, they always won (and occasionally broke) the hearts of Houstonians. They were authentic, full of talent, and had a "run and shoot" approach that made games exciting. When Adams couldn't get a stadium deal he liked, he moved the franchise to Tennessee in 1995. As much as we love the Texans, there is simply no replacing this H-Town institution.

Courtesy of Globe Ticket Company

Courtesy of Gerry J. Gilmore

HOUSTON COMETS

The Women's National Basketball Association has 12 teams, and attendance for games at each one was up by double-digit percentages in 2024. Started in 1997, the Houston Comets helped lay the foundation for the league. One of the original eight franchises, the Comets had a strong start by winning the first ever WNBA championship. The team attracted leading talent over the years, including Sheryl Swoopes, Cynthia Cooper, Tina Thompson, Janeth Arcain, and Kim Perrot—delivering a winning record overall. After struggling financially, however, the clock ran out on the Comets after the 2008 season.

Houston Hotshots

Indoor soccer is niche but fun if you have an open mind: The games are high-scoring (unlike the Premier League) and fast-paced; you're right next to the action; players can bounce the ball off of the walls, resulting in some crazy play; and it has a casual, high-energy vibe. From 1994 to 2000, the Houston Hotshots were our team in that scene. The Hotshots, which drew thousands of fans every time they played, originally competed in the Continental Indoor Soccer League before spending a few years in the World Indoor Soccer League. They had a rough first year but gained momentum—going 18-10 in both 1996 and 1997. By 2001, however, investment had dried up, and they got the red card for good. There was a shot at bringing them into the Premier Arena Soccer League 2015–2017, but it didn't work out.

Courtesy of Joshua Hoehne

Houston Buffaloes

The Buffs were a minor league baseball team (1896–1961) that played in the Texas League. Houston had minor league teams dating back to the Reconstruction days, with crazy team names like the Stonewalls and the Mud Cats. But the Buffaloes were relatively big time, becoming a farm team for the St. Louis Cardinals and a legitimate gateway to the majors. The Buffs brought Houstonians fun nights out, great baseball, trash-talking rivalries, and a cast of many colorful characters. The team was bought by the Houston Sports Association to clear the way for the Colt .45s in 1961.

Courtesy of Bain News Service

Houston Aeros

Houston actually had two Aeros hockey teams: one between 1972 and 1978 and another that resurrected the Aeros name between 1994 and 2013. The '70s World Hockey Association team, which played in the Sam Houston Coliseum and the Summit, garnered a ton of talent, including Canadian hockey legend Gordie Howe. But it was plagued by money problems, and the franchise died after the summer of 1978. In the mid-1990s, the next-generation Aeros were an American Hockey League team eventually affiliated with the Minnesota Wilds. Astronomical rent at the Toyota Center would run them out of town after the 2013 season.

Ticket courtesy of Richard Bartlaga

Photo courtesy of Todd Carr

INDEX

Interior of the Co-Cathedral of the Sacred Heart

Courtesy of Antony-22 via Wikimedia Commons
https://creativecommons.org/licenses/by-sa/4.0/deed.en